An Outline of

NEW TESTAMENT SURVEY

By

WALTER M. DUNNETT

*To Sharon and Mark
and their mother*

MOODY PRESS
CHICAGO

Printed in the United States of America

TABLE OF CONTENTS

CHAPTER   PAGE

1. The Background of the New Testament........ 7
2. The New Testament: Introduction........... 14
3. The Historical Literature of the New Testament.. 18
4. The Gospel of Matthew..................... 23
5. The Gospel of Mark....................... 32
6. The Gospel of Luke....................... 36
7. The Gospel of John....................... 46
8. The Book of Acts......................... 54
9. The Pauline Epistles: Eschatological........... 69
10. The Pauline Epistles: Soteriological........... 81
11. The Pauline Epistles: Christological...........104
12. The Pauline Epistles: Ecclesiological...........122
13. The Jewish-Christian Epistles: Hebrews
    and James 134
14. General and Personal Epistles: Peter—Jude.....147
15. The Prophetical Literature: Revelation.........163
    Index of Persons and Places.................173
    Index of Authors........................175

MAPS AND CHARTS

The Roman Empire (1st Century A.D.)........ 12
The Books of the New Testament............. 15
A Harmony of the Ministry of Jesus........... 22
Palestine in the Time of Christ............... 26
The Missionary Journeys of Paul.............. 60
Map of Paul's First and Second Journeys........ 62
Map of Paul's Third Journey................. 64
An Analysis of the Letters to the Seven
    Churches of Asia.......................168
The Three Series of Judgments...............170

ACKNOWLEDGMENTS

Acknowledgment is made to the following publishers for permission granted to quote from their publications: Baker Book House, *New Testament Commentary: I and II Timothy and Titus,* by W. Hendriksen, 1957; Wm. B. Eerdmans Publishing Co., *Commentary on the Gospel of Luke,* by N. Geldenhuys, 1956; *Commentary on the Epistles to the Ephesians and Colossians,* by E. K. Simpson and F. F. Bruce, 1957; *The New Testament: An Historical and Analytic Survey,* by M. C. Tenney, 1953; Harper & Brothers, *The Scrolls and the New Testament,* edited by Krister Stendahl, 1957; The Wartburg Press, *The Interpretation of St. Paul's Epistles to the Colossians, to the Thessalonians, to Timothy, to Titus, and to Philemon,* by R. C. H. Lenski, 1937; *The Interpretation of the Epistle to the Hebrews and of the Epistle of James,* by R. C. H. Lenski, 1938; The Westminster Press, *Introducing the New Testament,* by A. M. Hunter, 1946.

While the contributions of many in past days have gone into the making of this volume, special thanks are due to three individuals: Dr. Merrill C. Tenney, Dean of the Graduate School, Wheaton College, my former professor, who introduced me to the vast possibilities of the synthetic approach to the New Testament; Dr. J. C. Macaulay, a present colleague, who read part of the manuscript and gave advice and encouragement; and my wife who typed the final draft and saw to it that deadlines were met.

WALTER M. DUNNETT

PREFACE

THE MESSAGE OF THE NEW TESTAMENT is essentially one. It centers about the Person of Christ and the work of the cross. Christ appears *historically* in the Gospels, *mediately* in the Acts, *doctrinally* in the Epistles and *prophetically* in the Revelation. Redemption is *enacted* in the Gospels, *proclaimed* in the Acts, *interpreted* in the Epistles and *consummated* in the Revelation. This evangel is not a new one. "To him bear all the prophets witness, that through his name everyone that believeth on him shall receive remission of sins" (Acts 10:43, A.S.V.).

This book is intended for students at the beginning of their college or Bible institute study of the New Testament. For this reason the various chapters which follow attempt to give an overview of the entire collection of twenty-seven books. The brief treatment of background and the integration of the various segments of the New Testament should aid in attaining this aim. The purpose of the volume is to make clear the general content of the various books, not to deal primarily with matters of criticism or particular analysis. Finer points in the treatment of the books have been placed in footnotes. The suggested readings at the end of each chapter will provide opportunity for further investigations in the problem areas.

Unless otherwise specified, the text used is the Testament of the American Standard Version, 1901. Because of its greater accuracy it is quoted in place of the Authorized (King James) Version.

SUGGESTED READINGS
New Testament Commentaries

Alford, H. *The Greek Testament*. Revised by E. F. Harrison. Two double vols. Chicago: Moody Press, 1958.
———— *The New Testament for English Readers*. Chicago: Moody Press, n.d.

Buttrick, G. A., et al. (eds.) *The Interpreter's Bible*. Twelve vols. New York: Abingdon, 1951-1957. Vols. VII-XII. Liberal viewpoint; thorough treatment.

Davidson, F., Stibbs, A. M., and Kevan, E. F. (eds.) *The New Bible Commentary*. Grand Rapids: Wm. B. Eerdmans Publishing Co., 1953. Pages 771-1199.

Lange, J. P. (ed.) *Commentary on the Holy Scriptures*. Twenty-four vols. Grand Rapids: Zondervan Publishing House, 1956 (reprint). Volumes 15-24.

Lenski, R. C. H. *Commentary on the New Testament*. Twelve vols. Columbus, Ohio: Wartburg Press, 1933-43.

Nicoll, W. R. (ed.) *Expositor's Greek Testament*. Five vols. Grand Rapids: Wm. B. Eerdmans Publishing Co., n.d.

Robertson, A. T. *Word Pictures in the New Testament*. Five vols. New York: Harper & Brothers, 1933.

Stonehouse, N. B. (ed.) *The New International Commentary on the New Testament*. Seventeen vols. Grand Rapids: Wm. B. Eerdmans Publishing Co., 1951—. Now in process of publication. Thorough; conservative viewpoint.

Vincent, M. *Word Studies in the New Testament*. Four volumes. Grand Rapids: Wm. B. Eerdmans Publishing Co., 1957 (reprint).

CHAPTER 1

THE BACKGROUND OF THE
NEW TESTAMENT

A MID THE STREAM OF HISTORY in the pre-Christian era flow three main currents. One was primarily *religious* in nature, the Hebrew; another was chiefly *cultural,* the Greek; the third was predominantly *political* and *social,* the Roman. Each of these made its peculiar contribution to the world of that day.

The Hebrew Background

While the story of the Hebrew people might be traced from the time of Abraham, the period between the Babylonian captivity and the reign of the Herods is especially significant for the purposes of this study. The Diaspora[1] achieved something which had not been realized previously: the dissemination of the knowledge of Jehovah among the nations.

In 63 B.C. Palestine was subdued. Pompey entered Jerusalem and even invaded the Temple, much to the horror of the Jews. Except for a short rule by the Parthians (41-37 B.C.), the eastern enemies of Rome, Jerusalem was constantly under Roman dominion until the fall of the empire. During the years that followed, Palestine was governed by rulers appointed by Rome. The Gospels and Acts tell of the deeds and misdeeds of a number of these men, notably the family of the Herods and Pontius Pilate.[2]

---

[1]The Greek term used to describe the Jews who were "scattered abroad" throughout the ancient world. Josephus testified that Jews were to be found in "every place" (*Antiquities* 14, 115).

[2]Herod the Great ruled over Galilee as "King of the Jews" from 37 to 4 B.C. Matthew 2 records his attempt on the life of the Baby Jesus. Herod's son Archelaus ruled from 4 B.C. to A.D. 6 in Judea and Samaria. Another son, Herod Antipas, was tetrarch of Galilee from 4 B.C. to A.D. 39. It was

Wherever the Jew went he carried with him two great truths of his faith: *monotheism* and *the Law,* his ethical standard for living. Not only were these ideas propagated by word of mouth but when the Old Testament was translated into Greek (called the Septuagint) about 250-150 B.C., this knowledge also became available to all who could read.

Another factor establishing Judaism among the nations was the rise of the synagogue, possibly originating as early as the sixth or fifth century B.C. Both in cities of Palestine and in Gentile lands this meeting place' for reading of the Scriptures, prayer and worship appeared. To the Jew away from the Temple in Jerusalem it was a center of gathering; to the surrounding peoples it was a constant witness to the name of Jehovah.

Within the land of Palestine particularly the Second Temple was the great symbol of the unity of the faith. This center of worship was carefully guarded from all defilement, especially the presence of Gentiles. So it was that the invasion of the Holy Place by Antiochus Epiphanes of Syria, a thorn in the side of the Jew, set off the struggle for Jewish independence (168 B.C.). The years 165-63 B.C. saw varying degrees of freedom. Finally the Roman Pompey subjugated Jerusalem and the land in 63 B.C., and never again, until twenty centuries had passed, were the Jews free from oppression and foreign rule.

The chief sects of Judaism during the two centuries or so before the birth of Christ were the Sadducees (descendants of Zadok?) and the Pharisees (the "separatists"). The Sadducees were the priestly party and controlled the political fortunes of their people (under the eye of the Roman government). While this sect was smaller in number than the Pharisees, they made up for their numerical deficiency by their wealth and influence with their overlords. Theologically, they were opposed to the supernaturalism of their rivals (cf. Matt. 22:23; Acts 23:8) and gave greater importance to the books of the Pentateuch

he that Jesus called "that fox" (Luke 13:32) and the one responsible for the death of John the Baptizer. The Book of Acts records the reigns of the last of the Herods, Agrippa I, king of Judea from A.D. 37-44 (Acts 12), and Agrippa II, tetrarch of Chalcis and territories north and east of Judea from A.D. 48-70 (Acts 25, 26). Pontius Pilate, the procurator of Judea from about A.D. 27 to 37, was the Roman official who gave the death sentence in the "trial" of Jesus (John 18, 19).

than to the remainder of the Old Testament. The Pharisees, often referred to in the Gospels, were religious leaders, orthodox in their theology, holding to the entire Old Testament canon, the existence of angels and spirits, the resurrection of the body at the last day and immortality. The most noted Pharisee in the New Testament is, of course, Saul of Tarsus (Phil. 3:5, 6; Acts 26:5; 23:6).

An indication of the hopes and aspirations of the people of Israel in the days "between the Testaments" may be perceived in the writings denoted as "apocryphal" ("secret," "hidden") and "pseudepigraphal" ("false writings," those falsely credited to persons of note). These books, about twenty-five in number, were not accepted by the Jews as canonical. While not on a par with the Old Testament, they recorded aspects of the history, thought and future expectations of the people. The days of oppression under Syria, Antiochus IV in particular, called forth a renewed expression of devotion to Jehovah and a longing for the redemption which the Messiah would accomplish.

The Greek Background

Over three hundred years before the birth of Christ a son was born to Philip, king of Macedon. This boy, Alexander, was destined to be the greatest military figure the ancient world had seen. Before he had reached the age of twenty, Alexander, called the Great, set out to conquer the world. And conquer he did! From Macedon in the West to the Indus River in the East the young monarch laid claim to the wealth of lands and the minds of men alike. The Book of Daniel speaks of a he-goat who came from the west compassing the whole earth, and as he went did not touch the ground (8:5). This is a fitting description of the lightning-like movements of Alexander.

His contributions to the world were principally two: the Greek *culture* and the Greek *language*. One by one the nations fell before him; the armies of Persia, Phoenicia and Egypt tasted defeat at his hands. He established Greek cultural centers as he went. Many cities named "Alexandria" appeared in the wake of his conquests. The Greek way of life was adopted by people everywhere. The Greek language gradually became the lingua franca of the world and provided an ideal instrument for sounding the "Good News" which was yet to come.

The influence of Alexander produced the culture denoted as Hellenism, a name given to the Greco-Oriental way of life which was characterized by finesse, temperance and notable achievements in such fields as art, science, politics and philosophy. People of varying backgrounds and ways of life adopted a new mode of thinking and living—the Greek. They took on the customs, the dress and the language of Hellas. Alexander's dream of "one world" was realized to a great degree through the influences of factors such as these.

Prominent in Greek culture were the philosophies dating from approximately the sixth century B.C. From Thales of Miletus to the Stoics and Epicureans, the Greek mind reached out to discover the basic secrets of life and the universe.

Plato, considered by many to be the greatest mind in the ancient or modern world, taught that this world and all that it contained was at best only a shadow or a collection of individual representations of great eternal realities. The "Ideas" found their expression in the "ideas"; the spiritual could be dimly perceived amid the temporal; the "One" was the basis for the many.

By way of contrast, Aristotle, Plato's greatest pupil, taught that reality resided with the individual things themselves, not outside, as Plato had said. Characterized by "universal learning," Aristotle was an expert in nearly every branch of human knowledge. His writings exerted great influence on Christian thought, especially after the thirteenth century, as Plato's did during the Middle Ages.

By the time of the New Testament, however, the greatest days of classical philosophy were over. The Stoic and Epicurean schools (Acts 17) were mainly concerned with lesser issues. The former, founded by Zeno in the third century B.C., emphasized living according to nature and endurance in the face of the vicissitudes of daily existence, and promised an afterlife consisting of re-absorption into the all-encompassing World Soul. Epicurus, a contemporary of Zeno, and his followers, gross materialists who denied the idea of a future life, emphasized the simple life, the pursuit of pleasure and the avoidance of pain. When this life was concluded man, being wholly composed of atoms—body and soul—simply disintegrated and no longer existed as an entity.

Along with the philosophical speculations in these ancient days, the mystery religions offered their answer to the problems of life. Men and women, dissatisfied with the prevailing state religion which was impersonal and formalistic and longing for redemption from fear and frustration, turned to the mysteries to seek relief. Due to their esoteric nature, comparatively little is known of their rites and ceremonies. Being of Greco-Oriental origins they had a wide appeal. The god of the cult, patterned after the natural rhythm of the seasons, was one who had died (winter) and risen again (spring) and offered salvation to those who entered into a personal relation with him. The Eleusinian mysteries of Greece, the cult of Cybele of Asia Minor (a female figure), Adonis of Phoenicia, Serapis of Egypt and Mithras of Persia were the leading contenders for men's affections. With the possible exception of Mithraism, the rites of these cults were attended by immorality and debauchery in the name of religion.

The Roman Background

A new world power asserted itself in the Mediterranean world in the second century B.C.—Rome. Her military steam roller first flattened Carthage, then Greece, then moved on over Asia Minor. By the time Christ was born Augustus Caesar controlled the entire Mediterranean Basin.

The historical relationships existing between Roman officialdom and the Jews of Palestine are best depicted in the New Testament by Luke in the third Gospel. The relevant passages are three:

1:5 ff.—It is during the kingship of Herod the Great that Zacharias, the officiating priest, receives the announcement of the birth of a son, John.

2:1 ff.—It is during the reign of the emperor Caesar Augustus (27 B.C.-A.D. 14) that Joseph and Mary make their way to Bethlehem of Judea and Jesus the Christ is born (cf. Micah 5:2).

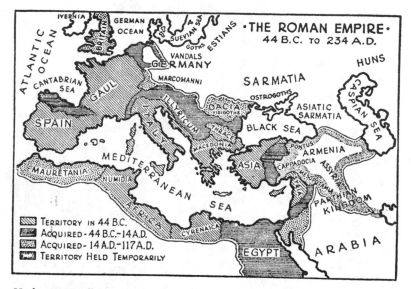

Herbert Newell Couch & Russel M. Geer, *Classical Civilization: Rome.*
Copyright 1940, 1950 by Prentice-Hall, Inc., Englewood Cliffs, N.J. By
permission of the Publisher.

3:1 ff.—It is in the fifteenth year of the reign of Tiberius
Caesar (A.D. 14-37) and in the days of the procuratorship of
Pontius Pilate (A.D. 27-37) that John the Baptizer begins his
preaching in the wilderness of Judea.

While Roman rule was outstanding in many respects, two
features were particularly significant for the rise of Christianity:
the *law* and the *order* of the empire (Pax Romana), and the
system of roads which made travel more easily possible, safer
than ever before. As Christian missionaries of the first century
went out, beginning at Jerusalem, the relatively peaceful conditions and the excellent roads were clearly aids to progress. It is
further noteworthy that the Roman attitude toward Christianity,
thought to be a part of Judaism, was one of friendliness or at
the worst indifference (cf. Acts 18, Gallio) throughout the first
generation of the history of the Church as depicted in the Book
of Acts.

Suggested Readings

Barrett, C. K. *The New Testament Background: Selected Documents.* London: S.P.C.K., 1957. (U.S. Distributors: New York: Macmillan). Source readings from Roman, Greek and Jewish writers with editorial comments.

Bruce, F. F. *Second Thoughts on the Dead Sea Scrolls.* Grand Rapids: Wm. B. Eerdmans Publishing Co., 1956.

Fairweather, W. *The Background of the Gospels or Judaism in the Period Between the Old and New Testaments.* Edinburgh: T. & T. Clark, 1926.

Manley, G. T., (ed.) *The New Bible Handbook.* Chicago: The Inter-Varsity Fellowship, 1953. See Part Three: "Toward Christ's Coming," pp. 265-297.

Metzger, B. M. *An Introduction to the Apocrypha.* New York: Oxford University Press, 1957.

Perowne, S. *The Life and Times of Herod the Great.* Nashville: Abingdon Press, 1957.

Pfeiffer, C. F. *Between the Testaments.* Grand Rapids: Baker Book House, 1959. Helpful survey of the period from Cyrus to Herod. Bibliography of primary source material.

Pfeiffer, R. H. *History of New Testament Times.* New York: Harper & Brothers, 1949. Detailed treatment of the period from 200 B.C. to the New Testament era, including an introduction to the Apocrypha.

Sauer, E. *The Dawn of World Redemption.* Grand Rapids: Wm. B. Eerdmans Publishing Co., 1952. Chapter XII, "The Fulness of the Time," pp. 175-186, is a concise summary of the pre-Christian era.

Snaith, N. H. *The Jews from Cyrus to Herod.* New York: Abingdon Press, 1956.

Tenney, M. C. *The New Testament:An Historical and Analytic Survey.* Grand Rapids: Wm. B. Eerdmans Publishing Co., 1953. See Part I: "The World of the New Testament," pp. 33-143. Excellent material and full bibliography.

CHAPTER 2

THE NEW TESTAMENT: INTRODUCTION

T HE MAIN THEME of the Bible is *redemption*. Beginning in Genesis it runs throughout the Bible. The New Testament continues the story of God's dealings with men begun in the Old Testament. Matthew is the beginning of the second great division of this story.

Christ is the central person of the Bible. While He appears prophetically in the Old Testament, He is incarnate in Matthew as "Jesus Christ, the son of David, the son of Abraham" (1:1). The record of His life and the lives of His followers is given in the succeeding pages of the New Testament.

In the Old Testament the chief emphasis is upon the divine Law. In the New Testament the stress is upon divine Love manifested in the Lord Jesus Christ. "Herein was the love of God manifested in us, that God hath sent his only begotten Son into the world that we might live through him" (I John 4:9). According to the Epistle to the Hebrews, Christ is "the mediator of a better covenant" (8:6). He came to reveal God and to declare God's will to mankind. Because He spoke the words of God, He was able to say, "The word that I spake, the same shall judge him in the last day" (John 12:48).

The New Testament, then, is the record of God's new covenant with men. His terms are clearly expressed. Man may accept this or reject it, but God's standards remain. Because it is a covenant there are obligations incumbent upon both parties.[1]

---

[1]The word "covenant" is a translation of the Greek term *diatheke*, which may mean "a will" or "a testament." Its usual New Testament meaning, however, is "a covenant," with reference to an arrangement or agreement between two parties which has definite conditions attached thereto and, once accepted by one party from the hand of another, is binding upon both.

The New Testament consists of twenty-seven books, varied in character. Of the total number, five are *historical,* twenty-one are *epistolary* and one is *prophetical.* Among the epistolary literature, fifteen are primarily *doctrinal,* while six are *personal.* The accompanying chart divides the various books according to these categories.

The Books of the New Testament

Literary Classifications	*Names of Books*	*Writers*
Historical (5)	Matthew Mark Luke John Acts	Matthew Mark Luke John Luke
Epistolary (21)	Romans I Corinthians II Corinthians Galatians Ephesians Philippians Colossians I Thessalonians II Thessalonians I Timothy ⎫ II Timothy ⎬ personal Titus ⎭ Philemon	Paul (13)
	Hebrews James I Peter II Peter I John II John ⎫ III John ⎬ personal Jude	Unknown James Peter (2) John (3) Jude
Prophetical (1)	Revelation	John

The historical period covered in these books spans about one hundred years (6 or 5 B.C.-A.D. 95). About fifty years was the length of time during which the books were written (A.D. 45-95). At least eight men had a part in writing the New Testament. If Hebrews is not a Pauline book there were nine. All the writers, with the possible exception of Luke, were Jews. Three of the men, Matthew, John and Peter, were disciples of Jesus, associated with Him during His earthly life. Two of the others, James and Jude, were brothers of Jesus (Matt. 13:55).

Within the New Testament itself are early indications of the esteem in which certain of the books were held by the Church. In I Timothy 5:18, quotations from the Book of Deuteronomy and the Gospel of Luke are both called "the scripture." II Peter 3:15, 16 states that Paul's writings are considered on a par with "the other scriptures." As the apostles considered the Old Testament to be the Word of God (II Tim. 3:15, 16; II Peter 1:21), the equating of these books with the Old Testament is a powerful witness to their rank in the early Church.

Not only are these writings described in this way, but they, as the Old Testament, have a practical outlook. The Scriptures are both "inspired of God and profitable." They are meant to reach man where he is. God has spoken, thus revealing His love. When the reader responds to the message his life is changed. The end result is described as attaining "unto the unity of the faith, and of the knowledge of the Son of God, unto a full-grown man, unto the measure of the stature of the fullness of Christ" (Eph. 4:13).

Suggested Readings

Blaiklock, E. M. *Out of the Earth: The Witness of Archaeology to the New Testament.* Grand Rapids: Wm. B. Eerdmans Publishing Co., 1957. One of the volumes in the paper-bound Pathway Series.

Bruce, F. F. *Are the New Testament Documents Reliable?* London: Inter-Varsity Fellowship, 1950. (U.S. Publisher: Eerdmans.)

———. *The Books and the Parchments.* London: Pickering & Inglis, Ltd., 1953 (revised edition). Good bibliography.

Orr, J. "The Bible" in the *International Standard Bible Encyclopedia.* Grand Rapids: Wm. B. Eerdmans Publishing Co., 1939. Volume I, pp. 465-467.

Scott, E. F. *The Literature of the New Testament*. New York: Columbia University Press, 1932. Written from a liberal standpoint.

Scroggie, W. G. *Know Your Bible*. Vol. II: Analytical. *The New Testament*. London: Pickering & Inglis, Ltd., n.d.

Thiessen, H. C., *Introduction to the New Testament*. Grand Rapids: Wm. B. Eerdmans Publishing Co., 1948.

Twilley, L. D. *The Origin and Transmission of the New Testament*. Grand Rapids: Wm. B. Eerdmans Publishing Co., 1957. One of the volumes in the paper-bound Pathway Series.

CHAPTER 3

THE HISTORICAL LITERATURE OF THE NEW TESTAMENT

COVERING A PERIOD of over sixty-five years (6 or 5 B.C.-A.D. 61 or 62), the four Gospels—Matthew, Mark, Luke and John—tell the story of the earthly life of Christ, and the Book of Acts relates the beginnings of the Christian church.

The Four Gospels

While the Gospels deal with a common subject—the "good news" concerning the birth, life, death and resurrection of Jesus Christ—the glimpses which they give differ in certain respects. The first three, Matthew, Mark and Luke, are called "synoptic" as they "view together" or take the same point of view of their Subject. These brief works place the emphasis on the fact that Jesus was "a man among men"; One who "went about doing good, and healing all that were oppressed of the Devil; for God was with him" (Acts 10:38). Howbeit, He was not only Man but was called "Emmanuel" ("God with us") in Matthew 1:23; "the Son of the Most High," in Luke 1:32; "the Christ, the Son of the living God" in Matthew 16:16. When John pens his record of this One he begins immediately with a declaration of His essential nature by affirming "the Word was God" (John 1:1). This emphasis is continued throughout the fourth Gospel, coming to its climax in the declaration of Thomas in 20:28, "My Lord and my God."

Not only are there these particular emphases regarding the Person of Christ but also the distinct areas of His ministry are described. In the Synoptics the chief locale is Galilee, the area in the north of Palestine, while in John more attention is given to the Judean ministry.

The first three Gospels contain many of the miracles and

parables of Christ and emphasize His dealings with the masses of the people. John records no parables, only seven miracles (called "signs") and gives much space to Jesus' dealings with the "Jews" (the hostile element, especially the leadership). In addition, the fourth Gospel is notable for its "interviews"—conversations which Jesus holds with various individuals (see chapters 1, 3, 4, 5, 9 and 11 especially).

The Synoptic Problem

This brief analysis may serve to introduce the chief literary dilemma of New Testament historical literature—the Synoptic problem. How is it that the material in the first three books is in so many respects similar if the writings are independent of each other? On the other hand, why are there such frequent divergences in the reports of Jesus' ministry unless the writings are to some extent independent of each other? The student may readily refer to volumes dealing with New Testament introduction to investigate the details for himself.[1] A number of basic observations must suffice at this point.

First, it should be noted that each of the writers has *a distinctive purpose* in view as he writes. This is stated by each of the evangelists. Notice Matthew 1:1; Mark 1:1; Luke 1:1-4; John 20:31. Such would influence not only the content but the arrangement of the materials as well.

Second, the *written* Gospels were preceded by the *oral* Gospel. The preaching of the early Church contained a definite core of factual material relating to the life and ministry of Jesus. Notice the sermons in the Book of Acts (particularly Peter's message in Acts 10:34-43) and Paul's concise summary in I Corinthians 15:1-4.

Third, each book was directed toward *a certain readership*. Matthew writes primarily, though not exclusively, to Jews. In the same manner, Mark addresses himself to Romans, Luke to Gentiles (Greeks) and John to the universal Church. Both the choice and arrangement of materials, then, may well reflect the purpose and the destination of each book.

---

[1]See H. C. Thiessen, *Introduction to the New Testament* (Grand Rapids: Eerdmans, 1943), pp. 101-129; G. T. Manley, *The New Bible Handbook* (London: Inter-Varsity Fellowship, 1953), pp. 320-322.

Fourth, the use of *written sources* is not precluded by the fact of divine inspiration. Luke makes reference to this factor in the preface to his Gospel (1:1-4). As the records of the words of Jesus are the most similar element in the Gospels, the employment by the writers of existing documents is a likely possibility.

Along with the possible use of written sources should be included *the acquaintance of the writers with one another.* This would be quite feasible as the synoptists moved about in such cities as Jerusalem and Caesarea.

Finally, and most important, the *superintending ministry of the Holy Spirit* lay behind all the labors of the human writers. Peter testifies to this fact in relation to the writers of the Old Testament (II Peter 1:20, 21). Jesus told His disciples that the Holy Spirit, when He came, would "teach you all things and call to your remembrance all things which I have spoken unto you" (John 15:26). This does not mean a "dictation" method of transmitting truth, but rather a divine guidance which pays respect to human personality.

The History Continued

The Gospels conclude with the ascension of Jesus into Heaven (Luke 24:50-53; Mark 16:19, 20). As Luke writes the second treatise he summarizes these final incidents (Acts 1:1-11), then carries the story forward for about another thirty years. The action begins in Jerusalem, the center of Judaism and the home of the nascent Church, and concludes in Rome, the hub of the mighty Roman Empire.

With the bold strokes of an historian's pen, Luke depicts in terms of living events the first generation of the Christian Church. Great figures dominate the scene, notably Peter and Paul. But above and behind the movements of men is the sovereign working of God the Holy Spirit. The vitality of these days is not found in organization but in spiritual energy. Once and again "they were all filled with the Holy Spirit." This is the reason that the Church, born in humble beginnings, soon found a place "in Caesar's household" (Phil. 4:22).

The panorama of the Apostolic Age (A.D. 30-100) is basically threefold:[2]

1. The founding of the Christian Church among the *Jews*. *Peter* is the prominent person; *Jerusalem* the prominent city.

2. The founding of the Christian Church among the *Gentiles*. *Paul* is the prominent person; *Antioch* (of Syria) the prominent city.

3. The final *summing up* and organic *union of Jewish* and *Gentile* Christianity in one fixed, independent whole. *John* is the prominent person; *Ephesus* the prominent city.

Suggested Readings

Scroggie, W. G. *Know Your Bible. A Guide to the Gospels.* London: Pickering & Inglis Ltd., 1948. A thorough treatment viewing the Gospels synthetically, analytically, and Christologically. Extensive bibliography.

Tenney, M. C. *The Genius of the Gospels.* Grand Rapids: Wm. B. Eerdmans Publishing Co., 1951. Deals with the nature and basic message of the four Gospels.

Edersheim, A. *The Life and Times of Jesus the Messiah.* Two volumes. London: Longmans, Green, and Co., 1900. (U.S. publisher: Eerdmans.) A standard work in its field.

Machen, J. G. *The Virgin Birth of Christ.* New York: Harper & Brothers, 1932. A thorough examination and defense of the doctrine of the virgin birth.

Morgan, G. C. *The Crises of the Christ.* New York: Fleming H. Revell Company, 1903. A rich study of the seven great crises of Christ, from His birth to His ascension.

Morris, L. *The Lord from Heaven.* Grand Rapids: Wm. B. Eerdmans Publishing Co., 1958. One of the volumes in the paper-bound Pathway Series.

Sanday, W. *Outlines of the Life of Christ.* New York: Charles Scribner's Sons, 1912.

---

[2]P. Schaff, *The History of the Apostolic Church* (New York: Scribner's, 1853), pp. 185, 186.

A Harmony of the Ministry of Jesus

Gospel	The Period of Preparation	The Period of Public Ministry		The Period of Suffering	The Period of Triumph
		Opening	Closing		
Matthew	1:1–4:16	4:17–16:20	16:21–26:2	26:3–27:66	28:1-20
Mark	1:1–13	1:14–8:30	8:31–13:37	14:1–15:47	16:1-20
Luke	1:1–4:13	4:14–9:21	9:22–21:38	22:1–23:56	24:1-53
John	1:1–34	1:35–6:71	7:1–12:50	13:1–19:42	20:1–21:25

CHAPTER 4

THE GOSPEL OF MATTHEW

Introduction

MATTHEW'S GOSPEL is the link between the Old and the New Testaments. Thus its place at the beginning of the New Testament is most appropriate. To the Jewish reader it clearly reflected the great themes of the Hebrew Scriptures: the Law, Messiah, the prophetic writings, the Kingdom and the nation of Israel.[1]

From the introductory words the book makes its appeal to the Jew: "The book of the generation of Jesus Christ, the son of David, the son of Abraham" (1:1). This is a record of Christ, the Messiah, the anointed One (cf. Ps. 2:2; Isa. 45:1), who was descended from David (His royal ancestry) and Abraham (His human ancestry). Citations from and allusions to the Old Testament occur with great frequency; nearly every chapter contains one or more such references.[2]

Author

The first Gospel, in common with the three which follow, is anonymous. The earliest statement of the Church Fathers regarding its authorship is to be found in the writings of Papias in the second century. He stated that "Matthew put together the oracles [of the Lord] in the Hebrew language, and each one

---

[1]W. Graham Scroggie, A Guide to the Gospels (London: Pickering & Inglis, Ltd., 1948), p. 248.
[2]Ibid., pp. 267-272. Scroggie lists 53 citations and 76 allusions. Only chapters 6 and 28 are omitted from the listings. Even here, however, there is at least historical reference to the Old Testament as Solomon appears in 6:29. Much of the Hebrew Scriptures is seen to be "predictive in character, and Messianic in substance."

23

interpreted them as best he could."[3] Tradition is unanimous in ascribing the book to Matthew.

This relatively obscure member of the disciples of Jesus is named in Matthew 9:9-13. As a tax collector for the Roman government he was busy at his work when Jesus called him. Following this incident Jesus shared the hospitality of Matthew's home. In the parallel passages in Mark 2:14 and Luke 5:27 he is called "Levi." This was likely his Jewish name and "Matthew" his Christian name. Aside from these three passages his name appears only in the lists of the apostles (Matt. 10:3; Mark 3:18; Luke 6:15; Acts 1:13).

Date and Destination

The Gospel has been dated as early as A.D. 50 (C. C. Torrey) and as late as A.D. 90-95 (E. F. Scott). Probably the earlier date is closer to the truth than the latter. In alluding to the destruction of Jerusalem (24:15), Matthew gives no indication that it has yet occurred. Such a major catastrophe could hardly have been passed over in silence when dealing directly with the subject. Probably a date between A.D. 55-70 is satisfactory.

As has been noted in the Introduction, Matthew addressed himself primarily to a Jewish readership. The Gospel was early connected with the Church in Syrian Antioch and may have been addressed to the Grecian Jews of that city. The Gentiles, however, are not neglected by the writer. The visit of the Magi in 2:1-12 and the commission in 28:18-20, addressing the Gospel to "all the nations," testify to the scope of the message.

Purpose

In view of the basically Jewish character of Matthew, together with the opening statement (1:1), there appears to be a twofold purpose for the Gospel: 1) to connect the message of the Old Testament with the Gospel (i.e., the "good news") and 2) to demonstrate, especially on the basis of Old Testament prophecies, that Jesus of Nazareth is the Messiah, the king of

---

[3]"Fragments of Papias," VI, taken from Eusebius, *Historia Ecclesiae*, iii, 39. *The Ante-Nicene Fathers*, Vol. I, p. 155.

the Jews.[4] Both the teachings of Jesus and His works, particularly His death and resurrection, substantiate the claim that He is the Messiah. Together with these evidences appears the witness of God the Father to the Sonship of Jesus (3:16, 17; 17:5).

Outline

The basic literary structure of the Gospel may be plainly discerned by the fivefold repetition of the common phrase "when Jesus had finished" (7:28; 11:1; 13:53; 19:1; 26:1). This expression marks the end of each major section of the book and concludes some special presentation of the ministry of Jesus. These five sections are preceded by the introduction (1:1—4:11) and followed by the conclusion (28:16-20) to the Gospel. The Theme: Jesus of Nazareth, the King of the Jews.

I. The Introduction of the King   1:1—4:11
  1. His genealogy   1:1-17
  2. His birth and early years   1:18—2:23
  3. His forerunner, John   3:1-12
  4. His baptism and temptation   3:13-4:11

II. The Demands of the King   4:12—7:29
  1. The beginnings of His ministry in Galilee   4:12-25
  2. The Sermon on the Mount   5:1—7:29

III. The Deeds of the King   8:1—11:1
  1 The miracles of Jesus   8:1—9:39
  2. The commissioning of the Twelve   10:1—11:1

IV. The Program of the King   11:2—13:53
  1 A message to John   11:2-6
  2. A message to the multitudes   11:7-19
  3. A message to cities   11:20-24
  4. A prayer and invitation   11:25-30
  5. A message to religious leaders   12:1-45
  6. A message to His family   12:46-50
  7. The parables of the Kingdom   13:1-53

---

[4]Basic questions which Jews would ask are answered by Matthew: "Was Jesus of the lineage of David? Did He uphold the Law? Had He come to establish the Kingdom?" Scroggie, *op. cit.*, p. 255.

PALESTINE
— IN THE —
TIME OF CHRIST

V. The Destiny of the King   13:54—19:2
   1. The unbelief of His countrymen   13:54-58
   2. The death of John   14:1-12
   3. The growth of opposition   14:13—16:12
   4. The prediction of the Church   16:13-20
   5. The prediction of His death   16:21-28
   6. The teaching in view of the cross   17:1-27
   7. The discourse on greatness and
      forgiveness   18:1—19:1

VI. The Problems of the King   19:3—26:2
   1. A series of questions and answers   19:3—20:28
   2. The healing of the blind men   20:29-34
   3. The entry into Jerusalem   21:1-11
   4. The cleansing of the Temple   21:12-17
   5. The cursing of the fig tree   21:18-22
   6. The questions of the Jewish leaders   21:23—22:46
   7. The denunciation of the Pharisees   23:1-39
   8. The Olivet discourse   24:1—26:2

VII. The Death and Resurrection of the King   26:3—28:15
   1. The events leading up to the cross   26:3-75
   2. The trial before Pilate   27:1-26
   3. The crucifixion and burial   27:27-66
   4. The resurrection   28:1-15

VIII. The Final Commission by the King   28:16-20

Special Features

A number of emphases appear in Matthew which distinguish it from the other Gospels.

1. *The emphasis on the King.* Both by explicit statement and by implication, the Gospel stresses that Christ is the King. The following passages are prominent:

1:1-17   The "Son of David" and His genealogy
2:1-12   The visit of the Magi to see the "King of the
           Jews"
21:5   Only Matthew includes the phrase, "Behold,

thy King cometh unto thee," in the entry to Jerusalem

25:31-46   The Son of man is to "sit on the throne of His glory"

27:37   The inscription on the cross reads, "This is Jesus, the King of the Jews"

2. *The discourses.* In each of the five major divisions of the Gospels a major discourse appears. It seems that Matthew grouped his material carefully, as narrative sections are followed by a discourse in each case. Thus the Gospel becomes well suited for teaching purposes in view of this systematic pattern.[5]

a. *The Sermon on the Mount* (5:1—7:29). Jesus, addressing His words to the disciples (5:1, 2) sets forth basic spiritual principles which are to characterize the subjects of the Kingdom.

5:3-16   The subjects of the Kingdom described

5:17-48   The new righteousness and its relation to the Law of Moses

6:1—7:12   The new righteousness and its relation to motives and daily life

7:13-29   Concluding exhortations

While Jesus makes it clear that He has not come "to destroy the law" (literally, "abrogate" or "set aside"), He shows the basic meaning of the Law by interpreting the commandments. The recurring phrases, "Ye have heard that it was said . . . but I say unto you" (5:21, 22; 5:27, 28; 5:31, 32; 5:33, 34; 5:38, 39; 5:43, 44) illustrates Jesus' approach. Basically, the Law of God is directed at the *heart* of man, not simply his external acts. Only a personal relationship to Christ is able to secure the intended result (7:24-27).

b. *The commission to the Twelve* (10:1-42). To the disciples Jesus imparted His authority (10:1) and, after carefully instructing them, sent them out to preach and heal. On this first mission they were told to go only to "the lost sheep

---

[5]For a helpful discussion and an analysis of all the discourses see Scroggie, *op. cit.*, pp. 291-311.

of the house of Israel"; the Gentiles and Samaritans were not here included (10:5, 6). At the close of the Gospel, however, they were sent to "all the nations" (28:19).

c. *The parables of the Kingdom* (13:1-53). By means of varied, common figures, Jesus describes the Kingdom of Heaven[6] in terms of its *growth* and its *value*. Of the seven parables, the first four are concerned with the aspect of growth, the last three with value.

13:3-9	The sower and the seed
13:24-30	The wheat and the tares
13:31, 32	The mustard seed
13:33	The leaven
13:44	The treasure hidden in the field
13:45, 46	The pearl of great price
13:47-50	The net and the fish

d. *The meaning of greatness and forgiveness* (18:1-35). This discourse is prompted by two questions from the disciples (18:1, 21). Jesus illustrates the meaning of greatness by the attitude of a little child (18:3, 4) and forgiveness by the parable of a king and his servants (18:22-25). Again, as in the sermon of chapter 5, the inner attitude is contrasted with external pretense.

e. *The Olivet discourse* (24:1—25:46). The setting for this final discourse was the Temple in Jerusalem, and the content answers the disciples' three questions, "Tell us, when shall these things be? And what *shall be* the sign of thy com-

[6]The expression "the kingdom of heaven" (lit., "the kingdom of the heavens") is found only in Matthew. In a Gospel which is distinctively Jewish, it can best be understood as a euphemism, as the Jews hesitated to use the divine Name. Compare I Maccabees 3:50; 12:15. Many teachings in Matthew using the expression "the kingdom of heaven" appear in Mark and Luke in connection with "the kingdom of God" (cf. Matt. 4:17 with Mark 1:15; Matt. 13:11 with Luke 8:10). L. S. Chafer, *Systematic Theology* (Dallas: Dallas Seminary Press, 1948), Vol. VII, pp. 224, 225, argues for a distinction between the two expressions in such passages as John 3:3 and Matthew 5:20. See George E. Ladd, *Crucial Questions about the Kingdom of God* (Grand Rapids: Wm. B. Eerdman's Publishing Co., 1954), pp. 126, 127, for an explanation of Matthew 5:20 which obviates the difference between the two. Ladd, *ibid.*, pp. 122-124, states that Daniel 2:44; 7:13, 14 seem to be the Old Testament background for the kingdom concept, though this phrase as such does not appear before Christian times.

ing, and of the end of the world?" (24:3).[7] Mark and Luke also contain this discourse, although in briefer form. Matthew includes four parables (24:43—25:30) and the judgment scene (25:31-46) which are not found in the other Gospels. A suggested chronological analysis follows:

Main Events	Matthew	Mark	Luke
The coming of deceivers	24:4-6	13:5-7	21:8, 9
The rise of persecution	24:9-13 (14)	13:9-13	21:12-19
The destruction of Jerusalem[8]	24:15-28	13:14-23	21:20-24
The beginning of sorrows	24:7, 8	13:8	21:10, 11
[The great tribulation]	[24:15-28]	[13:14-23]	
The second advent: Gathering of the elect	24:29-31	13:24-27	21:25-27 (28)
Judgment of the nations	25:31-46		
Present warnings to the disciples	24:32—25:30	13:28-37	21:29-36

3. *The prediction of the Church* (16:13-20). Only Matthew among the Gospels makes mention of the Church. The Greek word *ekklēsia* (lit., a "called-out" group) appears three times in Matthew (16:18; 18:17, twice) and is the subject of a prediction by Christ. As Peter confesses His Messiahship and deity, Jesus replies, "Upon this rock I will build my church" (16:18). The figure of the foundation rock (or stone) is elaborated upon by Paul in I Corinthians 3:11 and Ephesians 2:20, and by Peter in I Peter 2:4-8. Following Matthew, the next occurrence of the term is in the Book of Acts.

4. *The fulfillment of Old Testament prophecy.* From the opening chapter of his Gospel, Matthew emphasizes the fact that Jesus by His coming fulfilled many of the predictions of

---

[7]Grammatically, the questions fall into only two parts, as "the sign of thy coming and of the end of the world" are one thought. This is brought out in the accounts in Mark 13:4 and Luke 21:7. In the minds of the disciples, the coming of Messiah and the end of the age were connected.

[8]The destruction of Jerusalem in A.D. 70 by the Romans may well have been the near reference of this prophecy. But obviously, because of the words of Matthew 24:29 ("immediately after . . ."), the destruction of the end of the age is prophesied and therefore the "Great Tribulation" should be added to the list following the "beginning of sorrows."

the Old Testament writers. There are twelve references to the fulfillment of the prophecies.[9] They divide into two groups and should be carefully observed.

1. Matthew 1:22; 21:4; 26:56
2. Matthew 2:15, 17, 23; 4:14; 8:17; 12:17; 13:35; 26: 54; 27:9

The former group is characterized by a fuller statement of the events which fulfilled the prophecies, as Matthew looks back on all the things which have taken place and connects them with the Old Testament; the latter are generally briefer statements. Both groups of references, however, seem to allude to "the design of God in His providence."[10]

Suggested Readings

Broadus, J. A. *Commentary on the Gospel of Matthew* in *An American Commentary on the New Testament.* Philadelphia: The American Baptist Publication Society, 1886.

Goodspeed, E. J. *Matthew: Apostle and Evangelist.* Philadelphia: John C. Winston Co., 1959.

King, G. H. *New Order: An Expositional Study of the Sermon on the Mount.* London: Marshall, Morgan & Scott, Ltd., 1943.

Morgan, G. C. *The Gospel According to Matthew.* New York: Fleming H. Revell Co., 1929.

Morgan, G. C. *The Parables and Metaphors of our Lord.* New York: Fleming H. Revell Co., 1943.

Plummer, A. *An Exegetical Commentary on the Gospel According to St. Matthew.* Grand Rapids: Wm. B. Eerdmans Publishing Co., 1953 (reprint).

Stonehouse, N. B. *The Witness of Matthew and Mark to Christ.* Grand Rapids: Wm. B. Eerdmans Publishing Co., 1959 (reprint).

---

[9] In Mark the similar reference occurs only once (14:49), in Luke four times (1:20; 4:21; 21:22; 24:44), in John eight times (12:38; 13:18; 15:25; 17:12; 18:9, 32; 19:24, 36) and in Acts three times (1:16; 3:18; 13:27).

[10] J. A. Broadus, *Commentary on the Gospel of Matthew* (Philadelphia: The American Baptist Publication Society, 1886), p. 12.

CHAPTER 5

THE GOSPEL OF MARK

Author

JOHN MARK, the disciple of the Apostle Peter, was named by Papias and later writers as the writer of the Gospel which bears his name. Although his name does not appear within the second book of the New Testament, Mark is not infrequently seen in the Acts and Epistles (Acts 12:12, 25; 13: 5, 13; 15:37-39; II Tim. 4:11; Col. 4:10; Philem. 24; I Peter 5:13). As it was his mother's home which was the scene of the prayer meetings of the Jerusalem Church, he would have had frequent contact with Matthew and John. Later, in Rome, he met Luke (Col. 4:10, 14). In addition, he was the cousin (not, as in the A.V., "sister's son") of Barnabas (Col. 4:10).

In A.D. 112, Papias cited Mark as "the interpreter of Peter." A comparison of Peter's sermon in Acts 10:36-43 with Mark's Gospel shows the former to be an outline of the life of Jesus which Mark has given in much greater detail.

Date and Destination

The date of Mark's Gospel is, to a degree, determined by one's view of the relation of Mark to Matthew and Luke. If the priority of Mark is maintained the tendency will be to place it earlier (toward, say, A.D. 50)[1] and to place Matthew and Luke later. According to Irenaeus (*Against Heresies,* III, 1, i), Mark wrote down what Peter had preached after the departure of Peter from Rome. If the word translated "departure" (*exodus*) is taken in the sense of "leaving" the city, an earlier date may be assigned, say before A.D. 60. If it means, however,

---

[1]W. G. Scroggie, *A Guide to the Gospels* (London: Pickering & Inglis, Ltd., 1948), maintains the priority of Mark, dating it about A.D. 50. He cites A. T. Robertson and others as dating the book between A.D. 46 and A.D. 56 (pp. 170, 171).

"death" (cf. Luke 9:51), then a date at least in the late sixties
would be required. On this basis, assuming the Gospel was
written before the destruction of Jerusalem, Thiessen dates
Mark about A.D. 67/68.[2]

According to tradition, Mark wrote his Gospel in Rome
and directed it principally to Roman readers. The continual activity of Christ which Mark relates would especially appeal
to a Roman audience. In addition, the Latinisms occurring in
the book (use of Roman words for coins, military terms and
such) would strike a familiar note.

Purpose

The title of the Gospel, "The beginning of the gospel [good
news] of Jesus Christ" (1:1), gives an indication of what the
writer is setting out to record. The key verse (10:45) amplifies
this title and gives a specific character to the narrative. On the
basis of these statements the following observations may be
made:

1. Mark's purpose was to show, in organized fashion, the
importance of the works—especially the redemptive work—of
Christ. Consequently, activity is stressed above formal teaching.

2. An active narrative, such as is found here, was for the
benefit of the practical-minded Roman readers.

3. From an apologetic point of view, the Gospel shows the
rising tide of animosity against Jesus as the Jewish leaders plot
His death.

Outline

As Matthew presented Christ as the King of the Jews, so
Mark emphasizes the truth that Jesus is the Servant of Jehovah.
This is principally borne out by the picture of *continual activity*
which Mark depicts.

I.	Introduction	1:1
II.	Preparatory Events	1:2-13
III.	First Tour of Galilee	1:14—4:34
	Miracles and Parables	

---

[2]H. C. Thiessen, *Introduction to the New Testament* (Grand Rapids:Wm.
B. Eerdmans Publishing Co., 1948), pp. 145, 146.

IV.	Tour of Decapolis	4:35—5:43
V.	Second Tour of Galilee	6:1-29
VI.	Retreat to the Desert	6:30-52
VII.	Third Tour of Galilee	6:53—7:23
VIII.	Tour of the North Country	7:24—9:29
	First announcement of Passion	(8:31)
IX.	Fourth Tour of Galilee	9:30-50
	Second announcement of Passion	(9:31)
X.	Tour of Perea and Judea	10:1-52
	Third announcement of Passion	(10:33, 34)
XI.	Ministry in Jerusalem	11:1—13:37
XII.	The Passion and Resurrection	14:1—16:20

Special Features

1. In general, the two terms that might best describe the nature of the second Gospel are *conciseness* and *activity*. As to the former, it will be noted that Mark's over-all narrative is relatively brief, especially in comparison with Matthew or Luke, yet the manner in which he presents his facts does not suggest that he has overlooked pertinent aspects of Christ's ministry.

The activity in Mark is clearly depicted by the use of the Greek term *eutheōs* (or *euthus*) which is variously translated as "straightway," "immediately," "forthwith" or "anon." In all the word occurs forty-two times. Jesus is continually doing the will of His heavenly Father. The frequent employment of the Greek imperfect tense also adds to this sense of movement.

2. A notable feature of the Gospel is the large proportion of the narrative which is devoted to the Passion Week (the last week preceding the cross). This emphasis occupies about three-eighths of the entire book and shows that "the redeeming act is not Christ's life and teaching, but His death and resurrection."[3]

3. The number of miracles and parables is proportionately larger in Mark than in the other Gospels. There are about twenty miracles (in addition to the number of occasions where

---

[3]W. Graham Scroggie, *op. cit.*, p. 218.

He "healed many") and nearly that number of parables. The term "parable" appears about twelve times, although other parable-like illustrations occur.

4. If Matthew has painted a royal portrait of Jesus, Mark has presented a series of vignettes. His record might be described as a series of "picture glimpses" of his Subject in various situations and under differing circumstances, all designed to incite wonder and produce belief.

5. One strange feature in the story is the appearance of the unnamed young man in the Garden of Gethsemane the night of Jesus' betrayal (14:51, 52). Who was he? And why does he appear here? Church tradition suggests that Mark was the young man and was therefore an eyewitness to the events of that night. According to this story he has been called "stump-fingered" (*kolybodaktylos*) since he suffered the loss of his fingers by the slash of a Roman sword in the Garden.[4]

Suggested Readings

Alexander, J. A. *Commentary on the Gospel of Mark*. Grand Rapids: Zondervan Publishing House, n.d. (reprint).

Morgan, G. C. *The Gospel According to Mark*. New York: Fleming H. Revell Co.

Robertson, A. T. *Studies in Mark's Gospel*. Revised by H. F. Peacock. Nashville: Broadman Press, 1958.

St. John, H. *An Analysis of the Gospel of Mark*. London: Pickering & Inglis, Ltd., 1956.

Swete, H. B. *The Gospel According to St. Mark*. Grand Rapids: Wm. B. Eerdmans Publishing Co., 1956 (reprint). Advanced commentary. The Greek text with notes. Thorough introduction.

---

[4]A. M. Hunter, in *Introducing the New Testament* (Philadelphia: The Westminster Press, 1946), cites the illustration of Canon Streeter "that it was as if a reporter today were describing a shocking railway accident—the wild confusion, the telescoped carriages, the groans of the injured and dying —and were blandly to remark, 'Just then Mr. John Smith lost his pocket handkerchief.' Just so does the verse in Mark seem to us: it is pointless and inept unless it refers to John Mark himself; unless it is his own modest signature in the corner of his Gospel: his quiet way of saying, 'I was there'" (p. 34).

CHAPTER 6

THE GOSPEL OF LUKE

Introduction

YEARS AGO the French scholar Renan called this Gospel "the most beautiful book in the world." It is not difficult to discern the reason for such praise. The writer has presented a sublime picture of his Subject, the Son of man who came "to seek and to save that which was lost" (19:10). Throughout these pages "the human interest factor" is emphasized: the prominence of women and children, examples of prayer, songs, the careful recording of medical cases showing a physician's interest and many parables which grip and hold the reader's attention.[1]

Author

The writer of this Gospel was also the writer of the Book of Acts (cf. 1:1-4; Acts 1:1-5). Today few question that this man was Luke, doctor of medicine and close friend of the Apostle Paul. The tradition for Lukan authorship is early and consistent.

In Colossians 4:14 Paul calls Luke "the beloved physician"; in Philemon 24 a "fellow-worker"; and says in II Timothy 4:11, on the eve of his death, "Only Luke is with me." These statements should be put together with the "we sections" of Acts[2] which show that the writer of Acts was a companion of Paul during his various travels. Among the various companions of Paul, Timothy and the others mentioned in Acts 20:4, 5, must be ruled out as they went ahead of Paul and the writer on the trip from Philippi to Troas (Acts 20:6). Barnabas and Mark are mentioned in the third person in Acts; Jesus Justus

---

[1]For details see the material under Special Features.
[2]Acts 16:10-17; 20:5-21:18; 27:1-28:16. See also the discussion of authorship in chapter 8 (Acts).

was a Jew, while the writer of Acts was apparently a Gentile; Epaphras ministered in Asia (Colossians 4:12) rather than Macedonia; Demas deserted Paul (II Tim. 4:10). Luke remains as the best candidate. The absence of Luke's name in the record of Acts seems strange, unless he were the writer of the book.

Date and Destination

As the Gospel of Luke is the first part of a two-volume work, Luke-Acts, its date and destination are closely connected with the second volume. The Acts, closing with the statement of Paul's two-year imprisonment in Rome, is probably best dated about A.D. 62.[3] In view of this dating, Luke may be placed at A.D. 60, which fits in with the period of Paul's two-year stay at Caesarea. During this time Luke may well have done the actual writing of the story of the life of Christ.

This Gospel is addressed, first of all, to an individual, Theophilus, called by Luke "most excellent" (1:3). Of this man we know little. This honorary title, however, appears in Luke's writings elsewhere as an official appellation (see Acts 26:25) so that Theophilus may have been a Roman officer who had been previously introduced to the Christian message and was now the recipient of a full and orderly record of the life of Christ (1:4).

Beyond Theophilus, the book is destined for a Greek readership. Its presentation of "the Son of man" (the "ideal man") made its appeal to the Greek mind. Along with this emphasis should be included the human interest feature which is so frequently expressed, the many individuals who appear in the narrative, the stress on the universal nature of the Gospel and the fine style of Greek in which the book is written.

---

[3]It is likely that Acts was written soon after Paul's two-year imprisonment ended (Acts 28:30, 31). The friendly attitude of the Roman government clearly seen in Acts was not maintained after A.D. 64 when the Emperor Nero set out to persecute the Church. H. C. Thiessen and F. F. Bruce date the book in the early sixties. E. F. Scott dates it about A.D. 90, based on the idea that the writer did not make use of the Pauline epistles, which were in wide circulation in the Church by the end of the first century. The arguments for the early date, however, seem more in keeping with the content of the book.

Purpose

In the first four verses of the Gospel, Luke states succinctly the reason for his writing. It is that his friend Theophilus might know the certainty of the things in which he has been instructed.

Included in this preface, the only one of its kind in the New Testament, are a number of important statements which should be carefully studied.

1. Many persons had written down some record of the life of Christ. Apparently, for Luke's purpose at least, none of these was adequate (1:1-3).

2. Luke felt that he should provide for Theophilus another account of the earthly ministry of Christ and the story of the Gospel (1:3). He professes to have "traced the course of all things accurately" (1:3), which implies a good knowledge of the factual materials at hand. Paul uses the same word of Timothy who "followed" (lit., "traced") Paul's "teaching, conduct . . . what things befell me at Antioch, at Iconium, at Lystra" (II Tim. 3:10, 11).

3. Luke had traced these things "from the first" (1:3). The Greek word, *anōthen,* occurs thirteen times in the New Testament. In the writings of James and John the term usually means "from above." It occurs once again in Luke's writings (Acts 26:5) where it must mean "from the beginning," and once in Paul's (Gal. 4:9) where it is rendered "again" in the sense of "a second time, again." When a term is ambiguous, the usage of the writer himself (and of his companion, Paul) should be given preference if possible; therefore the rendering "from the first" is retained. (See the A.S.V. here.)

This statement gives us to understand, then, that Luke had an acquaintance with the facts which dated from an earlier time and that he also knew personally some of the persons who knew Christ firsthand. As in all the writings of Scripture, the Holy Spirit was the Guardian and Guide of all that was written.

4. Theophilus had been instructed beforehand (Gr., *katēchēthēs,* "catechized"); now Luke proceeds to establish him firmly in the things which he has been taught.

Outline

Luke presents Christ as "the Son of man." He is viewed as the ideal Representative of humanity and, as such, made an appeal to the Greek mind which thought in terms of the "universal man."

I. Prologue: The Purpose Stated   1:1-4

II. The Preparation of the Son of Man   1:5—4:15
   1. Annunciation to Zacharias   1:5-25
   2. Annunciation to Mary   1:26-56
   3. Birth of John   1:57-80
   4. Birth of Jesus   2:1-20
   5. Early years   2:21-52
   6. Preaching of John   3:1-20
   7. Final events   3:21—4:15

III. The Galilean Ministry of the Son of Man   4:16—9:50
   1. Announcement of His mission   4:16-30
   2. Introductory miracles   4:31—6:11
   3. Appointment of His disciples   6:12-19
   4. Beatitudes and instruction   6:20-49
   5. Miracles and parables   7:1—9:17
   6. Prediction of the cross   9:18-50

IV. The Perean Ministry of the Son of Man   9:51—18:30
   1. Challenge of discipleship   9:51-62
   2. Appointment of the Seventy   10:1-24
   3. Meaning of love   10:25-37
   4. Teachings of the Kingdom   10:38—13:21
   5. Rising opposition   13:22—17:10
   6. Final instructions   17:11—18:30

V. The Jerusalem Ministry of the Son of Man   18:31—21:38
   1. Journey to Jerusalem   18:31—19:28
   2. Entry into the city   19:29-44
   3. Problems of the ministry   19:45—21:4
   4. Predictions of judgment on Jerusalem   21:5-38

VI. The Passion Ministry of the Son of Man   22:1—23:56

    1. Last Supper and Gethsemane   22:1-46
    2. Betrayal, arrest and trials   22:47—23:25
    3. Crucifixion and burial   23:26-56

VII. The Resurrection Ministry of the Son of Man   24:1-53
    1. Empty tomb   24:1-12
    2. Emmaus disciples   24:13-35
    3. Appearance to the eleven   24:36-49
    4. Ascension   24:50-53

The opening events of the Gospel are closely connected with the current history of the day. When Zacharias received the announcement of the birth of his son, it was "in the days of Herod, king of Judea" (1:5). The time of the birth of Christ is linked with the days of Caesar Augustus (2:1), and the ministry of John begins "in the fifteenth year of the reign of Tiberius Caesar" (3:1). As an historian, Luke makes it clear that Christ entered the stream of human history under unique circumstances and at a crucial time. The days of Augustus Caesar were days of peace, prosperity and great opportunity. They were days in which religions flourished, yet were accompanied by deep spiritual longing. The hearts of the pious Jews longed for Messiah and His redemption of the nation. It was "in the fullness of the time" that "God sent forth his Son" (Gal. 4:4).

Jesus' birth was no ordinary one. Luke, with the use of great detail, recounts the events of the annunciation, Mary's conception by the Holy Spirit, Jesus' birth, and His early years, including the scene in the Temple (2:41-51). John comes as the forerunner of the Messiah in fulfillment of Isaiah's prophecy (Isa. 40:3 ff). Jesus is baptized by John, then sorely tested by Satan, but returns victorious "in the power of the Spirit" (4:14) to commence His public ministry in Galilee.

The Galilean ministry was begun with Jesus' dramatic announcement in the synagogue at Nazareth that He was God's "Anointed" (Messiah) and that His coming fulfilled Isaiah's prophecy of "the acceptable year of the Lord" (Luke 4:16-21). This appearance was followed with a number of miracles designed to confirm His lofty claims.[4] Following a night of prayer He chose and instructed His twelve disciples. After further miracles and teaching He predicted His coming death at the hands of His enemies.

For the most part 9:51—18:30 is peculiar to the third Gospel.[5] Jesus begins the journey from Galilee to Jerusalem (9:51) and in so doing passes through Samaria and Perea[6] before entering Judea. The emphasis of this section is Jesus' deliberate choice of the way to Jerusalem and the cross which awaited Him there.[7] In bold language Jesus sets forth the meaning of discipleship and then sends the Seventy on a preaching mission. He had earlier sent out the Twelve to preach the Kingdom of God and to heal (9:2); now the larger group is dispatched, two by two, to heal and announce the nearness of the Kingdom (10:9).

A number of notable parables occur in this section. Jesus teaches the meaning of love in the story of the Good Samaritan (10:25-37), prayer in the account of the importunate friend (11:5-13), the grace of God in seeking the lost in the three parables of chapter 15, the afterlife in the story of Dives and Lazarus (16:19-31), and true righteousness in the parable of the Pharisee and the publican (18:9-14).

With the dramatic announcement, "Behold, we go up to Jerusalem" (18:31), the final act of the drama commences. In successive steps the progress is marked out: 1) "Behold, we go up to Jerusalem . . ." (18:31-34); 2) "He went on before,

---

[4]Compare the similar approach in Matthew's Gospel where the claims of Jesus in the Sermon on the Mount (7:15-29) are followed by the miracles of chapters 8 and 9.

[5]N. Geldenhuys, *Commentary on the Gospel of Luke* in *The New International Commentary on the New Testament*, N. Stonehouse, editor (Grand Rapids: Eerdmans, 1956), p. 291: "This is in many respects the most important part of the third Gospel because the major portion of its contents does not occur in the three other Gospels."

[6]The so-called "Perean ministry" (see outline, IV) was not strictly confined to Perea, the area east of the Jordan River. In 10:38-42 Jesus appears in Bethany; in 17:11 He is at the borders of Samaria and Galilee. Possibly the entire passage could be described as a narration of events occurring between Galilee and Jerusalem.

[7]Geldenhuys, *op. cit.*, p. 293, footnote 1. Note the repeated allusions to the city of Jerusalem which occur in the chapters which follow: 9:51; 13:22; 17:11; 18:31; 19:28, 41.

going up to Jerusalem . . ." (19:28); 3) "He was now drawing nigh, *even* at the descent of the mount of Olives . . ."
(19:37); 4) "when he drew nigh, he saw the city and wept
over it . . ." (19:41); 5) "He entered into the temple . . ."
(19:45). In spite of the praises of the multitude as He entered the city, Jesus knew the condition of the hearts of the
people and wept over the city (19:41-44). Jerusalem, the center of Jewish religion is marked for destruction (21:20-24).

The Lukan account of the last events of Jesus' earthly life
is more detailed than either Matthew or Mark.[8] Among the
interesting incidents which only Luke records are the discussion about who was greatest among disciples (22:24-30),
the repentant thief on the cross (23:39-43), and the full story
of the Emmaus disciples (24:13-35), to which Mark only
alludes briefly (16:12, 13). The Gospel ends with the story
of the ascension of Jesus into Heaven (24:50-53) and this is
the point at which Luke resumes his history of Jesus in Acts.

Special Features

Professor N. B. Stonehouse has observed that a large part
"of the colour of Luke is derived from the singular and fascinat-
ing contents of the birth narrative, the parables and other
teaching in the middle chapters, and the account of the resurrection and the ascension of Christ."[9]

The following are the most outstanding of many Lukan
emphases:

1. *The infancy narrative* (1:5—2:52). Included here are
the annunciations to Zacharias, concerning the birth of his son
John, and to Mary, concerning the birth of her son Jesus. Along
with the detailed accounts of the births are included the hymns
of Luke's Gospel: the Magnificat by Mary (1:46-55); the
Benedictus by Zacharias (1:68-79); the Nunc Dimittis by
Simeon (2:29-32); the Ave Maria by Gabriel (1:28); and

---

[8]Matthew has 161 verses (26:1-28:20); Mark, 139 verses (14:1-16:20);
Luke, 180 verses (22:1-24:53). The final chapter of Luke gives a detailed
record of the events following Jesus' resurrection.
[9]*The Witness of Luke to Christ* (London: The Tyndale Press, 1951), p.
176. This volume (published in the U.S. by Eerdmans) is an excellent
analysis of the message of the third Gospel for the advanced student.

the Gloria in Excelsis by the angels (2:14). As has been noted previously, these accounts are placed in a definite historical setting (1:5; 2:1).

2. *The genealogy of Christ* (3:23-38). This is in the reverse order from Matthew (see Matt. 1:2-17) and traces Jesus' ancestry back beyond Abraham to Adam. Neither are the kings of Judah included here as they are in Matthew. The record is quite in keeping, therefore, with Luke's Gentile destination.

3. *The Emmaus road narrative* (24:13-35). The story clearly demonstrates the reality of the resurrection in the experience of two of the disciples of Jesus. Sadness gives way to joy as they realize who their Companion is.

4. *Miracles and parables.* There are six miracles and nineteen parables which are peculiar to Luke.[10] The six miracles are:

The draught of fishes	5:1-11
A widow's son raised	7:11-17
A woman with an infirmity healed	13:10-17
A man with dropsy healed	14:1-6
Ten lepers cleansed	17:11-19
Malchus' ear healed	22:49-51

Of the nineteen parables found only in Luke, the following are outstanding:

The good Samaritan	10:30-37
The prodigal son	15:11-32
The rich man and Lazarus	16:19-31

5. *The human interest features.* Of the many, small and large, the following incidents have a continual appeal:

Martha and Mary	10:38-42
Zacchaeus	19:1-10
The Emmaus disciples	24:13-35

The great abundance of personalities who are named, especially in chapters 1-3, add vividness and interest to the Gospel.

---

[10]See Scroggie, *A Guide to the Gospels,* p. 349, for list of contents peculiar to Luke.

6. *The prayers of Jesus.* There are seven occasions on which Jesus prayed which are found only in Luke:

At His baptism	3:21
Following a day of miracles	5:16
Before choosing His disciples	6:12
Before predicting His death	9:18
At the Transfiguration	9:29
Before teaching His disciples to pray	11:1
On the cross	23:34, 46

Luke places as much emphasis on prayer as the other Gospels combined. Matthew records three prayers, Mark four, John four, and Luke eleven.

7. *The Person and Work of the Holy Spirit.* Luke's two volumes are characterized by the doctrine of the Holy Spirit. In the Gospel He is active in the life of the Son of man; in the Acts He works through the apostles (Acts 1:2, 8). Some of the most important references in Luke are listed below:

Jesus—conceived by the Spirit	1:35
—attested by the Spirit	3:22
—led into the wilderness in the Spirit	4:1
—anointed by the Spirit	4:18
—rejoiced in the Spirit	10:21

Peter, in the Book of Acts, speaking of Christ's earthly ministry, says: "God anointed him with the Holy Spirit and with power: who went about doing good, and healing all that were oppressed of the devil; for God was with him" (10:38).

8. *A universal Gospel.* This book makes its appeal to people everywhere. It is not provincial. There are many expressions which show this outreach. The good tidings came to "all people" (2:10) and to "men" (2:14); salvation was prepared before the face of "all peoples" (2:31) and to "the Gentiles" (2:32); "all flesh" shall see God's salvation (3:6); the Samaritans are mentioned three times (9:54; 10:33; 17:16); Jesus came to seek and save "the lost one" (19:10); and the Gospel was to be preached to "all the nations" (24:47).

Suggested Readings

Geldenhuys, N. *Commentary on the Gospel of Luke* in *The New International Commentary on the New Testament*. Grand Rapids: Wm. B. Eerdmans Publishing Co., 1956. Good introduction and bibliography. Detailed commentary with special notes added.

Godet, F. L. *Commentary on the Gospel of Luke*. Grand Rapids: Zondervan Publishing House, n.d.

Luce, H. K. *The Gospel According to St. Luke* in the *Cambridge Greek Testament*. Cambridge: Cambridge University Press, 1933.

Plummer, A. *The Gospel According to St. Luke* in *The International Critical Commentary*. Edinburgh: T. & T. Clark, 1922.

Thomas, W. F. G. *Outline Studies in Luke*. Grand Rapids: Wm. B. Eerdmans Publishing Co., 1950.

CHAPTER 7

THE GOSPEL OF JOHN

Author

CLEMENT OF ALEXANDRIA (2d cent. A.D.) stated that John wrote "a spiritual gospel." The early Church Fathers agree with this statement of authorship. Only in recent years has there been an alternative suggestion made, based primarily on Papias' statement, which some have interpreted to mean that another than the apostle John authored the fourth Gospel.[1]

The classic statement in defense of the Johannine authorship, based on the testimony of the Gospel itself, was written by Bishop B. F. Westcott. Following is an adaptation of his four points:

1. *The writer was a Jew.* This may be gathered from his familiarity with the Old Testament (10:34, 35; 12:38-41; 19:24), his references to Jewish customs and religious observances (2:6; 10:22; 19:31) and the references to Jewish prejudices of one kind or another (4:9; 4:27).

2. *The writer was a Palestinian Jew.* He shows familiarity with Palestine and, in particular, the city of Jerusalem. Notice his references to Jacob's well in Sychar (4:5, 6), Solomon's porch (10:23), the pool of Siloam (9:7) and the praetorium (18:28). "There is every sign that the author was well acquainted with Palestine."[2]

3. *The writer was a contemporary and an eyewitness of the events recorded in the Gospel.* He begins and ends his narrative with a reference to his personal experiences (1:14; 19:35).

---

[1] Papias, a Church Father quoted by Eusebius (4th cent.), spoke of "John, a disciple of the Lord," and "the elder John." There is no good reason that the apostle John could not have been also called "elder" (cf. 1 Peter 5:1).

[2] E. F. Scott, *The Literature of the New Testament* (New York: Morningside Heights: Columbia University Press, 1938), p. 241.

Such apparently incidental notations as those found in 2:6; 6:10 and 21:11 look in the direction of an eyewitness account.

4. *The writer was John, the apostle, the son of Zebedee.* In the final chapter of the Gospel, the writer is identified with the beloved disciple (21:20) and is also a companion of the apostle Peter. His relationship to Jesus as "the disciple whom Jesus loved" is stressed at a number of crucial points in the narrative. At the scene in the upper room (13:23), at the trial of Jesus (18:15, 16) and at the crucifixion (19:26, 27), he appears in this role. The Synoptics refer on several important occasions to "the inner circle" of three, Peter, James and John. Of this number the first two are disqualified as possible writers, James by an early death (Acts 12:1, 2) and Peter by the fourth Gospel itself (21:20-24). As John is the best possibility remaining and, as he is traditionally so named, he is thereby accepted as the human author of the book which bears his name.

Purpose

Of all the Gospels, John contains the clearest statement of purpose. It occurs not at the beginning but near the end of the book and forms a fitting climax to all that has preceded.

> Many other signs therefore did Jesus in the presence of the disciples, which are not written in this book: but these are written, that ye may believe that Jesus is the Christ, the Son of God; and that believing ye may have life in his name.
>
> (20:30, 31)

Three words in particular are significant in this passage: *signs, believe* and *life.*

John's term to describe the miracles of Jesus—signs—emphasizes the spiritual meaning of the physical occurrence.[3] There is a total of seven miracles in the Gospel and, while they differ in kind, they are all designed to demonstrate the single truth that "Jesus is the Christ, the Son of God."[4]

---

[3] In the Synoptic Gospels the common words used to describe the miracles are "wonders" and "powers." The former stresses the effect on the people who viewed the miracle; the latter, the display of might which was evidenced.

[4] See pages 50-51 for a discussion of the seven signs and their witness to the person of Christ.

But "facts are stubborn things" and so John is not content to leave the reader with only a record of the deeds of Jesus. He desires that the reader will react in positive fashion to the evidence, that is, that he will *believe.*

What does it mean to believe? This question is amply answered by John, not in a formal statement as such, but by means of illustrations. It is significant that the noun "belief" never appears in the Gospel; it is always some form of the verb "to believe." Ninety-eight times the writer uses this word to show the reader what his response should be. He is to "believe on his name" (1:12); he is to "believe on him" (3:16); he is to "believe on him that sent" Jesus (5:24).

Along with the word "believe" occur a number of synonyms: "receive" (1:12), "drink" (4:14), "eat" (6:51), "come" (6:37), "enter" (10:9). By the inclusion of many individuals in the story John illustrates what it means to believe. People come to Jesus; some accept Him and follow with Him; others turn away, rejecting Him. Those who accept Him are "born again," "receive eternal life," "are not condemned," "have abundant life." Those who reject Him are "condemned," "shall perish," "remain in darkness."

The third important term is *life.* Going beyond simply physical life, this word has reference to the impartation of a new nature, an element which restores one to fellowship with God. This divine life comes to the person who places his trust in Jesus Christ, the Son of God, who died for him and rose again.

Outline

John presents Jesus as *the Son of God.* Taking this as the basic theme the outline is as follows:

    I. Prologue: The Presentation of the Son of God   1:1-18

   II. The Public Ministry of the Son of God   1:19—12:50
      1. Confronting individuals   1:19—4:54
      2. Confronting the multitudes   5:1—6:71
      3. Conflict with the multitudes   7:1—11:53
      4. Climax of the public ministry   11:54—12:50

  III. The Private Ministry of the Son of God   13:1—17:26

1. The Last Supper   13:1-30
2. The final discourse   13:31—16:33
3. The high priestly prayer   17:1-26
IV. The Passion Ministry of the Son of God   18:1—20:31
1. The betrayal   18:1-11
2. The trials before Annas and Pilate   18:12—19:16
3. The crucifixion and burial   19:17-42
4. The resurrection   20:1-31
V. Postscript: The Final Appeal of the
   Son of God   21:1-25

Contained in the Prologue are three basic features. First, the *leading character* of the Gospel is introduced. He is described as "the Word," "the Light," "Jesus Christ" and "the only begotten Son." He has come to give life to the world and to reveal God to men. Second, the *leading vocabulary terms* of the Gospel are introduced. Such words as "life," "light," "witness," "world" and "believe," which occur here, form a major part of the narrative that follows. Third, the *plot* of the Gospel is introduced. This is described as conflict between light and darkness, belief and unbelief. As the story progresses, this struggle becomes more and more pronounced until unbelief is climaxed with the cross and belief with the triumphant resurrection of Christ and the confession of Thomas, "My Lord and my God."

The public ministry of Christ occupies the first twelve chapters of the Gospel. One of the important features of this section is the contact which Jesus had with individuals. The disciples of John (chap. 1), Nicodemus (chap. 3), the Samaritan woman and the nobleman of Capernaum (chap. 4), all are confronted by the Person of Christ. John illustrates for his readers the ability of Christ to meet the spiritual needs of greatly differing kinds of people. In the chapters that follow, (5-12), the contacts with the multitudes and the religious leaders ("the Jews")[5] are emphasized. Beginning with the ac-

---

[5]The expression "the Jews" usually represents a hostile element in John's Gospel. It is the group which actively plots the death of Jesus in distinction from the multitude which is divided in its opinion concerning Him.

cusation that He is a Sabbath-breaker and a blasphemer (5:16-18), there is discernible a steadily mounting wave of opposition and conflict which eventuates in the rejection of Jesus by His own people (cf. 1:11).

Commonly called "the Upper Room Discourse," chapters 13-17 constitute a unique feature of the fourth Gospel. Here John records the last counsel of Jesus to His followers before the dark shadow of the cross falls upon Him. The discourse is concerned primarily with two things: His going away and the coming of the Holy Spirit. While He is personally absent from His disciples, the Spirit will be "another Comforter" and to them the source of strength and revelation. Chapter 17 contains the high priestly prayer of the Son as He commits Himself and His followers into the Father's hand.

The redemptive ministry of Christ is portrayed in chapters 18 through 20. Jesus knew "that his hour was come" and went forth to face His betrayer and those who would soon crucify Him. Following a detailed account of the trial before Pilate, John records the story of the death and resurrection of Christ which is the final episode in a narrative designed to call forth belief.

Why is chapter 21 now added? Is there anything yet remaining to be told? A confession of faith in Christ is to eventuate in a life of fellowship with and service for the living Lord. So Jesus challenges Simon Peter with the words, "Follow me." These were the words which described Peter's response to Jesus' first call (cf. Mark 1:18); now the words are uttered in a deeper sense, in the light of the example of Christ who demonstrated the meaning of devotion to God His Father.

Special Features

There are at least four features of John's Gospel which are worthy of special mention: the seven signs, the seven "I am's," the personal interviews and the portrayal of Jesus as God-man.[6]

1. *The seven signs.* Out of the many miracles which Jesus did (20:30), John recorded seven which are evidential in na-

---

[6]See further M. C. Tenney, *The New Testament: An Historical and Analytic Survey* (Grand Rapids: Eerdmans, 1953), pp. 201, 207.

ture. They are designed to picture for the reader that this man Jesus is the Messiah of Israel and the Son of God (20:31). As has been noted, the purpose of the sign is not to call attention to the physical act, primarily, but to teach a lesson of spiritual import. The following classification suggests the testimony of each sign to Jesus' person:

Name	Reference	Testimony
Changing water into wine	2:1-11	Power over quality
Healing the nobleman's son	4:46-54	Power over distance
Healing the impotent man	5:1-18	Power over time
Feeding the five thousand	6:1-14	Power over quantity
Walking on the water	6:16-21	Power over natural law
Healing the blind man	9:1-12	Power over misfortune
Raising of Lazarus	11:1-46	Power over death

2. *The seven I Am's.* Using seven natural figures, Jesus claims for Himself qualities which are clearly supernatural in character:

The Bread of Life	6:35
The Light of the World	8:12 (9:5)
The Door	10:7
The Good Shepherd	10:11, 14
The Resurrection and the Life	11:25
The Way, the Truth and the Life	14:6
The True Vine	15:1

In addition, the absolute use, "I am," occurs three times in chapter eight (8:24, 28, 58). The last of these, "Before Abraham was, I am," brought forth the accusation of blasphemy from the Jews (cf. Exod. 3:14) and they took up stones to kill Him.

3. *The personal interviews.* By this means John skillfully depicts the contacts of Jesus with those around Him. As people came face to face with Christ, they either accepted or rejected Him; belief or unbelief was exhibited. Tenney notes that there are twenty-seven interviews, some of which are extensive, others very brief.[7]

---

[7]*Ibid.* p. 207.

Among the interviews the most outstanding are with Nicodemus (chap. 3), the Samaritan woman (chap. 4), the blind man (chap. 9), and Martha and Mary (chap. 11). These all eventuate in belief. John also includes a detailed account of Jesus' trial before Pilate (chaps. 18, 19). A man apparently caught in a dilemma, Pilate yields to the pressure of his position and gives the order to crucify Jesus.

4. *The portrayal of Jesus as God-man.* While John's expressed purpose is to demonstrate that Jesus is the Son of God[8] no other Evangelist so clearly portrays the humanity of Christ. Both these emphases are stated in the prologue of the Gospel. "The Word was God" (1:1) and "the Word was made flesh and dwelt among us" (1:14). Even as Jesus claimed that "I and the Father are one" (10:30), and "no man taketh my life from me. I lay it down of myself that I might take it again" (10:18), He also was weary (4:6), He wept (11:35), He died and was buried (19:17-42). This same emphasis continues throughout the Gospel, climaxing in the confession of His deity by Thomas as He stands among His disciples following His resurrection from the grave (20:28).

In his Gospel, then, John has described a unique individual, One who calls forth personal faith and deep devotion. This is indeed "the Christ, the Son of God, *even* he that cometh into the world" (11:27).

Suggested Readings

Godet, F. L. *Commentary on the Gospel of John.* Grand Rapids: Zondervan Publishing House, n.d. Two volumes.

Hayes, D. A. *John and His Writings.* New York: Methodist Book Concern, 1917.

Hendriksen, W. *Exposition of the Gospel According to John* in *New Testament Commentary.* Two volumes. Grand Rapids: Baker Book House, 1953. Thorough introduction and commentary.

Macaulay, J. C. *Devotional Commentary on the Gospel of John.* Grand Rapids: Wm. B. Eerdmans Publishing Co. Penetrating spiritual insights into the words and works of Christ.

---

[8]The expression, "the only begotten Son" (John 1:18; 3:16) is to be understood in a qualitative sense, that is, "the only one of His kind." Christ is a unique individual. See J. H. Thayer, *A Greek-English Lexicon of the New Testament* (New York: American Book Company, 1889), p. 417.

Smith, D. *John* in *Commentary on the Four Gospels.* New York: Doubleday, Doran & Company, Inc., 1928.

Tenney, M. C. *John: The Gospel of Belief.* Grand Rapids: Wm. B. Eerdmans, 1948. An analytic approach to the fourth Gospel; includes detailed outline based on the paragraphs.

Thomas, W. H. G. *The Apostle John.* Grand Rapids: Wm. B. Eerdmans Publishing Company, 1946.

Westcott, B. F. *The Gospel According to St. John.* Grand Rapids: Wm. B. Eerdmans Publishing Co., 1951. A standard work, indispensable to the student of the fourth Gospel.

CHAPTER 8

THE BOOK OF ACTS

H ISTORICALLY, this is the most important book in the New Testament. Apart from the vital record which is contained in Acts, a great void would be left in the story of Jesus and the early church. Nearly all we know of the history of Christianity from about A.D. 30-60 has been given here in "the first church history." That which is contained in the New Testament and Epistles is basically a supplement to Acts.

Author

There are no serious doubts as to the authorship of this work. Nearly all scholars maintain that the writer of the third Gospel was also the writer of Acts and that he was Luke the physician. Together with adequate external testimony, the internal evidence for Lukan authorship is as follows:

1. *The preface to the Book of Acts.* The writer, addressing Theophilus (cf. Luke 1:3), makes reference to a "former treatise" which dealt with "all that Jesus began both to do and to teach until the day he was received up" (1:1, 2). This is an apparent reference to the third Gospel.

2. *The "we sections" in Acts.* In these sections of the book the writer includes himself in the narrative of Paul's journeys (16:10-17; 20:5—21:18; 27:1—28:16). It is known from Paul's Epistles that Luke was one of his companions in his missionary labors and during the Caesarean and Roman imprisonments (Col. 4:14; Philem. 23; II Tim. 4:11). As the style of these sections is similar to that of the other parts of Acts, it may be assumed that the same hand penned the whole volume. (For added details, see pages 36-37.)

3. *The medical terms of the book.* Both in the third Gospel and Acts there is the frequent use of medical terminology.

While this feature has been both championed (Hobart) and largely discounted (Cadbury), the frequency seems sufficient to assume the professional status of the writer, especially when viewed in the light of Luke's treatment of healing miracles and the fact that Paul calls him "the beloved physician" (Col. 4: 14).

Date and Destination

Little more need be said here than has already been noted in the treatment of Luke's Gospel.[1] The similar address and the notation of the "former treatise" and its relation to Acts (1:1, ff.) serve to unite the two books. (See further on pages 37, 38.)

Purpose

Generally speaking, the common purpose of the two volumes has been expressed in Luke 1:4. There are, however, a number of very specific aims which the writer accomplishes in Acts.

1. *The historical motive.* A comparison of Luke 1:1-4 with Acts 1:1-5 shows a continuing history. The subject of the former work is "the things which Jesus *began* to do and teach"; Acts shows the *continuation* of that work through the Holy Spirit in the lives of the apostles. The story is centered in the origin and expansion of the Church and is a portrayal of missionary strategy. From Jerusalem the Gospel spreads through Judea and Samaria and eventually reaches Rome. Both the power and the program are delineated in 1:8, the final words of Jesus before His ascension.

2. *The apologetic motive.* Addressing himself to the Roman world, Luke presented evidence to show that the Gospel enjoyed a pleasant reception at the hands of government officials. It is noteworthy, indeed, that in every contact with provincial governors, Christianity was either accorded a good hearing or, at the worst, ignored, but never opposed.[2] In chapter 13, Sergius

---

[1]R. B. Rackham, *The Acts of the Apostles* (London: Methuen & Co., Ltd., 1947), reviews the arguments for various datings of the book. His conclusion, based on good evidence, is that it must be dated not later than A.D. 64 (pp. viiia-viiic; l-lv). Further discussion and extensive bibliography is given by A. T. Robertson, "Acts of the Apostles," in the *International Standard Bible Encyclopedia*, Vol. I, pp. 39-48.

[2]Opposition is frequently met with in contacts with Jewish leaders. This is the source of trouble for the Church. See chapters 3-5, 6-9, 12 especially.

Paulus, the proconsul of Cyprus, "believed" the message of Paul; the officials at Philippi apologized for the rough treatment of Paul and Silas, which had been brought on by soothsayers (16:35-39); Gallio, at Corinth, simply ignored the missionaries (18:17); the Asiarchs of Ephesus (19:31) were sympathetic toward Paul and his mission and the "town clerk" came to the rescue of the Christians during the riot; Felix, Festus and Agrippa (24-26) all accorded Paul a sympathetic hearing and declared "he had done nothing worthy of death." In the face of increasing hostility toward the Church as the first century wore on, the record of Luke provided a sound defense for the Church and its message.

3. *The doctrinal motive.* Without question, the most outstanding doctrinal emphasis of Acts is the Person and Work of the Holy Spirit. This continues the characteristic theme of the third Gospel which stresses the ministry of the Spirit in the life of Christ.

Beginning with the promise of His coming (1:5-8), Luke traces His Advent and the accompanying events of the day of Pentecost (2:1-47). The transformed apostles bear witness in the power of the Spirit. As a result three thousand souls are saved and the Lord continues to "add to the church" daily. Not only is the Spirit's power evidenced in service, but also in discipline (5:1-11) when Ananias and Sapphira lied concerning their financial affairs. In this important passage the Holy Spirit is called God (5:3, 4). As the book continues He is active in giving wisdom (chap. 6), guidance (chaps. 8, 16) and calling people for particular service (chap. 13).[3] So it is that this book has been called "the Acts of the Holy Spirit."

4. *The biographical motive.* While Luke's record is primarily concerned with the chief events in the early days of the Church, he paints his pictures in terms of leading personalities. So pronounced is this feature that Acts may be divided into two major sections as "the Acts of Peter" (1-12) and "the Acts of

---

[3] A brief but suggestive analysis of the Spirit's varied ministries in Acts appears in J. C. Macaulay's *Life in the Spirit* (Grand Rapids: Eerdmans, 1955).

Paul" (13-28).[4] This book is a vivid illustration of the power and presence of God in human experience. The two leading apostles are men who are "filled with the Spirit" and who do what they do in the power of that Spirit. Whether in their private (10:19; 9:17) or public (4:8; 13:9) lives, this relationship is evident.

Luke's story throbs with the vigor of human life. As Peter makes his way to the house of Cornelius (chap .10), as Paul confronts the philosophers of Athens (chap. 17), as Stephen and Philip and James move about and play their part in God's program, the reader feels caught up "in the same bundle of life." It was through such as these that Jesus continued His ministry which was begun in the Gospel story.

Outline

Acts may be outlined in a number of ways. Two of the most natural are the *geographical* and the *biographical* approaches. For the sake of comprehensiveness these means are combined in the following outline. The key verse is 1:8, which sketches the geographical boundaries.

I. Introduction: The Apostolic Commission Given   1:1-11

II. The Gospel in Jerusalem: *Origins*   1:12—8:3
   1. The ministry of Peter   1:12—5:42
   2. The ministry of Stephen   6:1—8:3

III. The Gospel in Samaria and Judea:
    Transition   8:4—11:18
   1. The ministry of Philip   8:4-40
   2. The ministry of Saul begun   9:1-31
   3. The ministry of Peter concluded   9:32—11:18

IV. The Gospel in the Uttermost Parts:
    Expansion   11:19—21:14
   1. The ministry of Barnabas   11:19—12:25
   2. The ministry of Paul the apostle   13:1—21:14

---

[4]See especially R. B. Rackham, *The Acts of the Apostles*, (London: Methuen & Co., 1947). The volume excels in its treatment of personalities, events and places.

     a. The first journey   13:1—14:28
     b. The Jerusalem Council   15:1-35
     c. The second journey   15:36—18:22
     d. The third journey   18:23—21:14

   V. The Gospel in Caesarea and Rome:
      Imprisonment   21:15—28:29
     1. Paul taken prisoner in Jerusalem   21:15—23:10
     2. Paul as a prisoner in Caesarea   23:11—26:32
     3. Paul as a prisoner in Rome   27:1—28:29

  VI. Conclusion: The Apostolic Commission
      Fulfilled   28:30, 31

Luke reiterates the final message of his Gospel as he introduces the story of the early Church (cf. Luke 24:44-53; Acts 1:1-11). Before His ascension Jesus reminds His disciples of 1) the *promise* of the Father (1:4), 2) the *power* which would come upon them (1:8), and 3) the *program* for the Church (1:8). With these final words He vanishes from their sight.

The apostles were to wait in Jerusalem for the coming of the Holy Spirit and here it was that the Church was born. As had been the case in the Gospel record so here Peter was the leader and spokesman of the apostolic group. Some of his "sermons" are recorded in these early chapters together with his defenses before the Jewish Council (see chaps. 2, 3, 4, 5). The man who appears in these pages is a transformed man. He is no longer the fearful, cringing Peter of the night of Jesus' betrayal (Luke 23:54-62), but a bold, fearless preacher and apologete, "filled with the Holy Spirit."

Stephen joins Peter as a participant in these early days. He is a Hellenist,[5] one of the seven appointed to service in Acts 6, and a man described as "full of the Holy Spirit and wisdom" (6:3).[6] As he defends the Christian evangel before the Council, he becomes the first martyr of the early Church.

---

[5] A Hellenist was one who was by culture Greek though by birth a Jew, or at least non-Greek. This distinction stems from the days of Alexander the Great (see chap. 1) and separated these men from the Hebraistic (Palestinian) Jews, such as Peter and the other apostles.

[6] In Acts 6 is recorded the story of a problem involving the Hebraistic and Hellenistic widows in the church. The latter group felt that they were being neglected in the distribution of necessary provisions. The matter came to

It is at this point in the narrative that a significant person appears. At the scene of Stephen's death an apparently minor reference introduces the man who will become the chief character of the book. The men who stoned Stephen, says Luke, "laid down their clothes at the feet of a young man named Saul" (7:58). After hearing Stephen's dying testimony, that "I see the Son of Man standing on the right hand of God," Saul rages out against the nascent Church, launching the severe persecution alluded to in 8:1, ff. The believers are "scattered abroad throughout the regions of Judea and Samaria, except the apostles."

Following the history of the origin and growth of the Church in the confines of Jerusalem, Luke traces the transitional stage in its development, showing the Gospel in Judea and Samaria (8:4—11:18). For a brief period the focus of attention is turned on another member of the seven, Philip the Evangelist. Reaching out into Samaria, the region adjacent to Judea on the north, he evangelizes a people who "have no dealings" with the Jews (cf. John 4:9). When the report of his labors reaches the ears of the apostles in Jerusalem, they dispatch Peter and John to confirm the work. The bestowal of the Holy Spirit on these people shows the genuineness of their faith and their acceptance before God. Philip continues his ministry in the area of Gaza where he is instrumental in the conversion of the man of Ethiopia, treasurer under one of the queens of the Candace dynasty (8:27).

The second aspect of the transitional period is Peter's work along the western coast of Palestine, especially in the city of Caesarea (chap. 10). For the "apostle to the Jews" this was a difficult yet vital venture. The vision which he received in the house of Simon in Joppa was a divine directive to preach to a Gentile household. Laying aside his natural prejudices he went to Caesarea. Acts 10:34-43 is an abbreviated record of what he said; the following verses are a record of what God

---

the attention of the apostles and the result was the selection and appointment of "seven men of good report, full of the Holy Spirit and wisdom" to care for the needs of these women.

The Missionary Journeys of Paul

Refs.	Places Visited	Personnel	Main Events	Main Results

I
 	
Acts 13:4—
14:28
	Departure from Antioch (Syria)
	Seleucia
	Cyprus: Salamis
	    Paphos
	Pamphylia: Perga
	Galatia: Antioch
	    Iconium
	    Lystra
	    Derbe
	    and return to
	    Antioch (Syria)
		Paul
		Barnabas
		John Mark
			Contest with Elymas at Paphos
			Sermon in synagogue at Antioch
			    (Pisidia)
			Paul and Barnabas worshiped
			    at Lystra
			Paul preaches, then is stoned at
			    Lystra
				Conversion of Sergius Paulus at
				    Paphos
				Conversions and riot at Antioch
				    (Pisidia)
				Churches founded and established
				    in all Galatian cities; elders appointed
				Report of journey to the Church in
				    Antioch (Syria)

II
 	
Acts 15:36—
18:22
	Departure from Antioch (Syria)
	Syria and Cilicia
	Galatia: Derbe and Lystra
	Troas
	Macedonia: Philippi
	    Thessalonica
	    Berea
	Achaia: Athens
	    Corinth
	Asia: Ephesus
	Caesarea
	Return to Antioch (Syria)
		Paul
		Silas
		Timothy
		(Luke)
			Timothy added to party at Lystra
			Vision at Troas; Luke added to
			    party
			Preaching and imprisonment at
			    Philippi
			Preaching and persecution at
			    Thessalonica
			Preaching at Berea
			Sermon on Mars' Hill in Athens
			Eighteen-month stay at Corinth,
			    teaching, trial before Gallio
			Short stay at Ephesus, preaching
				Conversion of Lydia and the jailer
				    at Philippi, Church founded
				Church founded at Thessalonica
				Conversion of Dionysius and
				    Damaris at Athens
				Church founded at Corinth

III
 	
Acts 18:23—
21:14
	Departure from Antioch (Syria)
	Galatia and Phrygia
	Asia: Ephesus
	Macedonia
	Greece
	Macedonian cities
	Troas
	Asia: Melitus
	Syria: Tyre
	    Ptolemais
	Caesarea
	Jerusalem
		Paul
		Silas
		Timothy
		(Luke)
		Gaius
		Aristarchus
		Sopater
		Secundus
		Tychicus
		Trophimus
			Teaching ministry in Ephesus
			    (2-3 years)
			Riot of the Ephesian silversmiths
			Preaching at Troas
			Eutychus restored to life
			Farewell to the Ephesian elders
			    at Miletus
			Warning to Paul at Tyre regarding Jerusalem
			Warning to Paul at Caesarea by
			    Agabus regarding Jerusalem
				Church established at Ephesus;
				    center of evangelization of
				    Asia
				Instruction to the Ephesian elders
				    regarding official duties

did. The Gentiles received eternal life and the gift of the Holy Spirit and the transition was complete (cf. 11:1-18).

From 11:19 to 21:14, the key word is *expansion*. The chief character is Saul (later called Paul, the apostle; see 13:9), and the narrative centers about his gigantic missionary labors stretching from Syrian Antioch across the four provinces of Galatia, Asia, Macedonia and Achaia. Barnabas, Silas, Timothy and Luke are the most important of his numerous companions. Among his converts were Sergius Paulus, the proconsul of Cyprus (13:12), Lydia, a businesswoman of Philippi (16:14), the jailer of Philippi (16:32), Dionysius, one of the Athenian Aereopagites (17:34), and Crispus, ruler of the synagogue in Corinth (18:8).

Beginning with the ministry of Barnabas and Saul in 11:22-26, Antioch of Syria becomes the hub of Gentile Christianity. From this city these men are called by the Holy Spirit (13:1-3) and the missionary journeys of Paul occupy a major part of the remaining history in the book. The accompanying chart will illustrate the main lines of progress during this period.

On the first journey Barnabas and Saul, accompanied by youthful John Mark, left Antioch to evangelize Cyprus and parts of Asia Minor. The most important accomplishment of this venture was the founding of the Galatian churches (Acts 13, 14). Having traversed the island of Cyprus and the province of Pamphylia on the southern coast of Asia Minor, the missionaries entered Antioch (of Pisidia) in Galatia. Paul's sermon in the synagogue followed, climaxing in the declaration of "justification by faith in Christ and not by the works of the law" (13:38, 39).[7] When the unbelieving Jews roused persecution against them, Paul and Barnabas proceeded to Iconium (14:1-7) and then to Lystra (14:8-20).

The people of Lystra, seeing Paul heal a lame man, hailed the missionaries as gods "come down in the likeness of men." They called Barnabas, Jupiter (Zeus, the chief god of the Greek Pantheon) and Paul, Mercury (Hermes, the messenger god). In the light of the ancient legend that once before in the

[7]This, in germ form, is the message of the Galatian Epistle. (See esp. Gal. 2:16.)

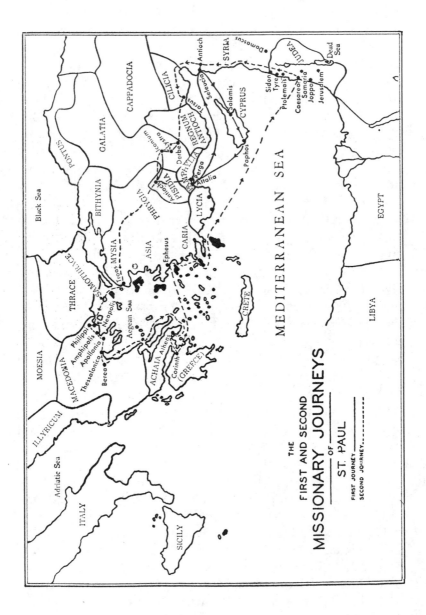

THE
FIRST AND SECOND
MISSIONARY JOURNEYS
OF
ST. PAUL

FIRST JOURNEY _____
SECOND JOURNEY -----------

MEDITERRANEAN SEA

history of Lystra these gods had visited the city, the excitement was understandable. Only with difficulty the pair convinced the people that they were simply messengers of the true God of Heaven. Hardly had this been accomplished when the Jews, inciting the crowd to violence, had Paul stoned, dragged from the city and left for dead. But, being raised up, Paul went back into the city and the next day departed for Derbe, a border outpost for Roman military forces. The return trip through these same cities resulted in the establishment of the churches and the appointment of elders.

It was to these churches that Paul later addressed his Epistle to the Galatians and their experience became a test case for Gentile freedom. The first Church Council (Acts 15) gathered to consider the question of the salvation of Gentiles. "Must a Gentile become a Jew before he can become a Christian?" The Judaizers maintained this doctrine (Acts 15:1), but Paul and Barnabas vigorously contested it. James, the brother of Christ and moderator of the Council, rendered the decision that no additional requirements were to be placed on Gentile believers; these new converts were to abstain from eating bloody meats or those consecrated to idols, and to maintain high moral standards so as not to offend their Jewish brethren. A report of the decision was then sent to the churches of Syria and Cilicia (15:22-29).

The second journey sees the departure of Paul and Silas into Asia Minor while Barnabas and his cousin John Mark return to Cyprus (15:36-41). Passing through the Galatian province, Paul picks up young Timothy at Lystra (16:3) and the three travel west and north. When they are prevented by the Holy Spirit from going either into Asia or Bithynia they come to Troas, a coastal city and the point of departure for Europe. The experience encountered at Troas may well be considered one of the most crucial in the history of Christianity. Following the call received from the "man of Macedonia," Paul and his companions pressed westward into Europe. Hence, in time, it was the Western world that received the Gospel and the accompanying blessings of Christianity.

As a result of Paul's labors in Macedonia and Achaia, the

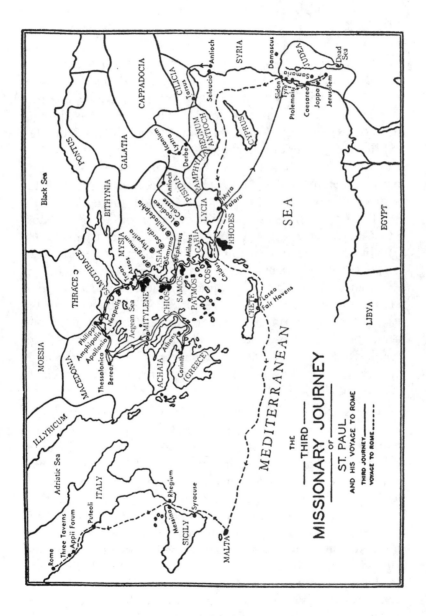

THE

THIRD

MISSIONARY JOURNEY

OF

ST. PAUL

AND HIS VOYAGE TO ROME

THIRD JOURNEY ————
VOYAGE TO ROME ------

churches at Philippi, Thessalonica, Berea and Corinth came into being. In Philippi the missionaries were accused of teaching customs "unlawful for Romans to observe" (16:20, 21), in Thessalonica of "saying that there is another king, *one* Jesus" (17:7); the Athenians accused Paul of seeming to be "a setter forth of strange gods" (17:18) and, in Corinth, one who "persuadeth men to worship God contrary to the law" (18:13).[8] Yet in all this God overruled and Paul saw great fruit as a result of this mission.

The third journey is concentrated primarily in the area of Ephesus, "the first city of Asia."[9] Paul spent over two years here carrying on an intensive evangelistic and teaching ministry (19:9, 10). That his efforts were not in vain may be readily observed as one reads his later message to the Ephesian elders (20:17-35), the Ephesian Epistle itself, the letters to Timothy at Ephesus and the final letter in Revelation 2:1-7. Following his stay in Ephesus were short visits to Macedonia, Achaia, Troas, Miletus and Caesarea. Finally, he made his way to Jerusalem with gifts for the poor of that church.

At this juncture the final stage of the narrative of Acts is reached (21:15—28:31). Paul is taken prisoner in Jerusalem, accused of defiling the Temple (21:27-36) and imprisoned in the Roman castle for safekeeping. He is then portrayed by Luke in various scenes making a defense of his position. Before the Jewish mob (22) and the Council (23) in Jerusalem, and the governors Felix (24) and Festus (25) and King Herod Agrippa II (26) in Caesarea, he affirms his innocency of the charges of subverting the Jewish religion (24:5, 6). His appeal to

---

[8]The accusations are particularly meaningful in the light of the political and religious character of these cities. Philippi was a Roman colony, hence closely tied to Roman law. Thessalonica was a free city and, while it had its own rulers (politarchs), it was eager to express its loyalty to its King, Caesar. The Athenians, surrounded by many gods, knew little of the Christian message, and interpreted "Jesus and the resurrection" to be two foreign divinities. In Corinth the Jews attempted to level charges of subversion against Paul, but Gallio the proconsul dismissed the case as purely a religious disagreement.

[9]This was the boast of Ephesus herself. At this date Pergamum, to the north, was still the capital of the Roman province. See Wm. Ramsay, *The Letters to the Seven Churches of Asia.* (London: Hodder & Stoughton, n. d.), p. 283.

Caesar, the privilege of every Roman citizen (25:11), took him to Rome after two years. The story of that voyage, a classic story of the sea, is told in the closing chapters (27, 28). While a prisoner under house arrest in Rome, the apostle continued "preaching the kingdom of God, and teaching the things concerning the Lord Jesus Christ" (28:31) for another two years. Thus ends Luke's narrative of the things that Jesus continued to do through His chosen servants.

Special Features

As Acts is the pivotal book of the New Testament, the question might well be raised as to its relationship to both the Gospels and the Epistles. The following observations should serve to clarify the issue.

1. *Acts continues the history begun in the Gospels,* especially that of Luke. The meaning and effect of the life, death and resurrection of Christ become increasingly clear to the reader of Luke's second volume.

2. *Acts records the origin of the Church* which is 1) *predicted* in the Gospels and 2) *expounded* in the epistles. The Church is alluded to in Matthew 16:18 and found functioning and well established from Romans through Jude; without the Acts, the origin of the Church would be an enigma. Where did it come from? Who were its early leaders? These and many other questions are answered in the chapters of Acts.

3. *Acts contains the historical background for many of Paul's Epistles.* A fuller appreciation for and understanding of Paul's writings will be gained by the careful student of Acts. Notice the following parallels:

Acts 13:14—14:28	First journey: Paul in Antioch, Iconium, Lystra and Derbe: Background for *Galatians*
Acts 16:11-40	Second journey: Paul in Philippi: Background for *Philippians*
Acts 17:1-9	Second journey: Paul in Thessalonica: Background for *I and II Thessalonians*
Acts 18:1-16	Second journey: Paul in Corinth: Background for *I and II Corinthians*

Acts 19:1-41   Third journey: Paul in Ephesus: Background for
Acts 20:17-35   Ephesians, I and II Timothy

4. Acts demonstrates the practical application of Christian doctrines recorded in the Epistles. Under this heading would be included teaching for believers both personally and corporately. The reality of the Spirit-filled life, the meaning of Christian fellowship, the appointment of Church officers and the care of the churches all come vividly before the reader of Acts. Its pages illuminate the principles penned by the apostles to the churches which they had founded.

"And they went forth, and preached everywhere, the Lord working with them, and confirming the word by the signs that followed" (Mark 16:20).

Suggested Readings

HISTORICAL BACKGROUND

Cadbury, H. J. *The Book of Acts in History.* New York: Harper & Brothers, 1955. Includes the Greek, Roman, Jewish and Christian environments of the first century.

Foakes-Jackson, F. J. and Lake, K., eds. *The Beginnings of Christianity.* Five volumes. London: Macmillan and Co., Ltd., 1920-1933. Volume I is especially helpful in its treatment of Jewish, Gentile and Christian backgrounds.

Goodwin, F. J. *A Harmony of the Life of St. Paul According to the Acts of the Apostles and the Pauline Epistles.* Grand Rapids: Baker Book House, 1953.

Purves, George T. *Christianity in the Apostolic Age.* Grand Rapids: Baker Book House, 1955. (Reprint of 1900 edition.)

Ramsay, W. M. *St. Paul the Traveller and the Roman Citizen.* Grand Rapids: Baker Book House, 1949. A study of Paul based on his experiences as recorded in the Book of Acts.

————. *The Church in the Roman Empire Before A.D. 170.* London: Hodder & Stoughton, 1908. Part I, pp. 3-168, deals with Paul's labors.

COMMENTARIES

Blaiklock, E. M. *The Acts of the Apostles: An Historical Commentary* in *The Tyndale New Testament Commentaries.* Grand Rapids: Wm. B. Eerdmans, 1959.

Bruce, F. F . *Commentary on the Book of the Acts* in *The New International Commentary on the New Testament.* Grand Rapids: Wm. B. Eerdmans Publishing Co., 1954. Excellent commentary. Thorough verse-by-verse treatment.

Macaulay, J. C. *A Devotional Commentary on the Acts of the Apostles.* Grand Rapids: Wm. B. Eerdmans Publishing Co., 1946.

Moorehead, W. G. *Outline Studies in the New Testament: Acts to Ephesians.* Grand Rapids: Baker Book House, 1953.

Morgan, G. C. *The Acts of the Apostles.* New York: Fleming H. Revell Company, 1924.

Rackham, R. B. *The Acts of the Apostles.* Thirteenth Edition. London: Methuen & Co., Ltd., 1947. Highly recommended.

CHAPTER 9

THE PAULINE EPISTLES: ESCHATOLOGICAL

Introduction

THE GREATEST SINGLE FIGURE of the early Church is Paul the apostle, and his writings number at least thirteen among the Epistles of the New Testament. If Hebrews is Pauline, the number comes to fourteen. Before giving detailed consideration to these books, attention should be directed to 1) the writer, 2) the classification of the writings, and 3) a suggested chronology of the life of Paul.

1. *The writer.* A convenient threefold division of Paul's life would be his preconversion days, his conversion experience and his postconversion days. On the basis of the history given in Acts and the scattered references in Paul's Epistles, the following picture emerges.

Saul, born in the city of Tarsus, was a man of varied background. He was a Jew by birth and training; culturally he was Greek (Hellenist); by citizenship he was Roman (Phil. 3:5, 6; Gal. 1:13, 14; Acts 21:39; 22:3, 28; 26:4, 5). A promising student of the Scriptures and Rabbinic lore under the noted Rabban Gamaliel[1] in Jerusalem, Saul had outstripped most of his fellow-students and was capturing the attention of his superiors. It is possible, though not certain, that he was a member of the Sanhedrin, the supreme governing body of Judaism. At any rate, as the chief enemy and most active persecutor of the Church, he had the right to cast his official vote against

---

[1] The title "Rabban" is used of Gamaliel in *The Mishnah* (translated by H. Danby), Sotah, 9:15. He was the first of seven eminent rabbis to be given the designation. See Conybeare and Howson, *The Life and Epistles of St. Paul* (London: Longmans, Green, and Co., 1898), pp. 47, 48. As a title of respect it occurs twice in the Gospels, addressed to Jesus (Mark 10:51; John 20:16), rendered "Rabboni."

the accused.[2] As has been noted previously in the Book of Acts, Saul was present at and gave consent to the stoning of Stephen. Believing that the Christian affirmation of the Messiahship, resurrection and exaltation of Jesus of Nazareth was a falsehood, he set out to exterminate this blasphemy against his Jewish faith.

It was in such a state of mind that Saul made his way to Damascus (Acts 9:1, ff.) to seize further victims. With the suddenness of a lightning bolt, a great light from Heaven struck him to the ground and blinded him. When Saul heard the answer to his question ("Who art thou, Lord?"), "I am Jesus whom thou persecutest," the awful truth dawned on him. Stephen had been right! He, Saul, had been wrong! His mind recalled that fateful day; it was hard for him to kick against the goad. His response was unequivocal: "What shall I do, Lord?" The will of the persecutor was yielded to a new Master, and Saul of Tarsus was commissioned as a preacher and an apostle.

Following a brief period in Damascus (Acts 9:20-22), a stay in Arabia (Galatians 1:17) and fifteen days in Jerusalem, Saul returned to his home in Tarsus. Here he remained until Barnabas sought him out and brought him back to Antioch to aid in a teaching ministry in the Church in that city (Acts 11:25, 26). From Antioch as a base of operations he carried on his missionary labors for about ten years. During these years six of his Epistles were written (Romans, I and II Corinthians, Galatians, I and II Thessalonians). After his imprisonments in Jerusalem and Caesarea he was taken to Rome and there wrote four other epistles (Ephesians, Philippians, Colossians and Philemon). In the last years of his life, probably as a free man for a short time and then as a prisoner again, he penned I and II Timothy and Titus. According to tradition, he was executed near the end of the reign of Nero in the city of Rome as a martyr for his faith.

From his first appearance to his last, Paul is portrayed as a

---

[2]In Acts 26:10, the literal rendering is "I dropped in my [black] pebble against them." This was a vote of condemnation and gives the background for our modern term "blackballed."

man of intense zeal and determination. His devotion, first to
Judaism, then to Christ and the Gospel, is unmatched. Sensing
his own unworthiness in the light of his blood-stained past, he
yet rejoiced that he had received mercy and that God had
"counted him faithful, appointing him to *his* service" (I Tim.
1:12). Commissioned as "the apostle to the Gentiles," he yet
retained a great heart for his own people (Rom. 9:1-3; 10:1).
The chief emphases of his message may be found in such passages as Galatians 2:16-20; Romans 1:16, 17; Philippians 3:
1-16 and Titus 2:11-13.

2. *Classification of his writings.* On the basis of a combined
chronological-doctrinal organization, Paul's epistles may be
classified as follows:[3]

a. *Eschatological Epistles:* I and II Thessalonians. These
books deal with the last days and emphasize the return of Christ.
While they may or may not be the earliest of Paul's Epistles,
they are among the most far-reaching in time. Notice especially
II Thessalonians 2, which pictures the Day of the Lord and the
coming of Antichrist.

b. *Soteriological Epistles:* I and II Corinthians, Galatians
and Romans.

This group of letters have a common emphasis: the doctrine
of salvation. In the Corinthian Epistles, it is salvation applied
in the life of the Church; in Galatians, it is salvation by faith
as opposed to works; in Romans, it is salvation logically developed in the areas of justification and sanctification and applied
to sinful man, whether Jew or Gentile.

Thus Paul shows that "salvation" reaches beyond that which
a person receives by an act of faith in the Lord Jesus Christ;
it has its basis in the righteousness of God; its price is the blood
of Christ; it is received by faith and the individual is thereby
justified, called upon to live a life of dedication to God and to
apply this new life to his personal and corporate relationships.
It touches the religious, social, political and personal aspects
of day-by-day experience.

[3]An exact chronological arrangement is, of course, impossible at the present state of knowledge. There is, however, general agreement among scholars
as to the order of writing, the Epistle to the Galatians being the outstanding
exception. See pages 72-73 for further chronological details.

c. *Christological Epistles:* Philemon, Colossians, Ephesians and Philippians.

Also called the Prison Epistles, these books lay emphasis on the person and work of Christ. The personal note written to Philemon regarding his slave, Onesimus, illustrates the principle of divine forgiveness through imputation. Colossians and Ephesians, the twin Epistles of the New Testament, both deal with Christ and His Church. The stress of Colossians is that Christ is the Head of the Church; in Ephesians, the Church is the Body of Christ. Philippians, Paul's most personal Church Epistle, emphasizes the humiliation of Christ in His incarnation and His consequent exaltation. Applying His example to himself, the believer finds the secret of true joy in his own experience.

d. *Ecclesiological Epistles:* I Timothy, Titus and II Timothy.

The last letters written by the apostle are concerned with the organizational aspects of church life. I Timothy and Titus combine personal instruction to two apostolic delegates with requirements for church officers. II Timothy, Paul's final Epistle, emphasizes diligence and faithfulness in view of coming spiritual declension. Together the three are called the Pastoral Epistles.

3. *Chronology of the life of Paul.* The main events of Paul's career are fairly well marked out in Acts and the Epistles, although the dates given below are necessarily approximate.

A.D. 33   Conversion (Acts 9, 22, 26; Gal. 1:13-16)

33-35   Period spent in Damascus, Arabia and Jerusalem (Acts 9: 19-29; Gal. 1:15-20)

35   Return to Tarsus in Cilicia (Acts 9:30)

45   Ministry with Barnabas in Antioch of Syria (Acts 11:25, 26)

46   Second visit to Jerusalem: famine relief (Acts 11:27-30; 12:25; Gal. 2:1-10)

47-48   First missionary journey: Cyprus, Perga, Antioch of Pisidia, Iconium, **Lystra and Derbe** (Acts 13, 14)

(49)   Galatians, written from Antioch of Syria[4]

49/50   Third visit to Jerusalem: Church Council (Acts 15:1-35)

50-52   Second missionary journey: Cilicia, Galatia, Troas, Philippi, Thessalonica, Berea, Athens, Corinth, Ephesus (Acts 15: 36—18:22)

(50/51)   I and II Thessalonians, written from Corinth

53-56   Third missionary journey: Cilicia, Galatia, Ephesus, Macedonia, Greece, Philippi, Troas, Miletus, Caesarea (Acts 18: 23—21:14)

(55/56)   I Corinthians, written from Ephesus; II Corinthians, from Macedonia; Romans from Corinth

57   Arrest in Jerusalem (Acts 21:27 ff.)

58-60   Two years' imprisonment in Caesarea (Acts 23:31—26: 32)

60   Voyage to Rome (Acts 27, 28)

60-62   Two years' imprisonment in Rome (Acts 28:30, 31)

(60/61)   Philemon, Colossians, Ephesians, Philippians written from Rome

62-67   Release and further travels

(64/65)   I Timothy, Titus—place of writing uncertain

67   Final imprisonment in Rome

(67/68)   II Timothy, written from Rome

67/68   Martyrdom

I THESSALONIANS

Authorship

In contrast to the historical books, which are anonymous, the Epistles in most cases begin with the name of the writer. This is so in all of the recognized Pauline Epistles.

I Thessalonians contains the name of the author in 1:1 and 2:18. Notice also the frequent allusions to Paul's journey which took him to Thessalonica and beyond (1:5; 2:1, 2; 5-11, 13; 3:1-6). The external evidence is likewise clear. In the second century it was included in the list of Marcion (A.D. 140), Mura-

---

[4]Galatians may be dated later. Ramsay dates it A.D. 53; Lightfoot, A.D. 57. See the discussion in Chapter 10 under "Galatians."

torian Canon (A.D. 170), and quoted by name by Irenaeus (A.D. 180).[5]

Date and Destination

On the second journey Paul crossed the Aegean Sea from Troas to Philippi (Acts 16). After this, together with Silas and Timothy, he came to Thessalonica (Acts 17:1-9) and immediately began his preaching in the synagogue. Luke states that he "reasoned with them from the Scriptures" (17:2), which is the first recorded occurrence of this approach in the Pauline preaching in Acts.[6] They were described as those "who have turned the world upside down" (17:6).[7] Having begun their preaching, they were accused of saying that "there is another king, Jesus" (17:7). Before long the party was forced to leave the city and Paul, after a short visit in Berea (17:10-13), proceeded to Athens (17:15-34) and then Corinth (18:1-17). From the last city he wrote this epistle and it may be dated A.D. 50/51.

Thessalonica, still a thriving metropolis today (Saloniki), was in Paul's day the capital of the province of Macedonia, and had the rank of a free city. It therefore had its own government officials (politarchs) and was jealous of its status.[8] The cry raised against the apostolic preaching (see above) would seem to be an evidence of their "loyalty" to Caesar, their real sovereign. As in many cities of the day, idolatry was rampant. Paul makes reference to this fact when he reminds his readers how they "turned to God from idols, to serve the living and true God" (1:9).

---

[5]G. Milligan, *St. Paul's Epistles to the Thessalonians* (London: Macmillan and Co., Ltd., 1908), p. lxxiii.

[6]See further 17:17 (Athens): 18:4 (Corinth); 18:19; 19:8, 9 (Ephesus); 20:7, 9 (Troas); 24:12, negative (Jerusalem).

[7]Moulton and Milligan, *The Vocabulary of the Greek Testament* (London: Hodder & Stoughton, Ltd., 1952), p. 38, cite two first-century instances of the term. The more famous is in a boy's letter to his father in which he reports that his distraught mother has said of him, "He quite upsets me—off with him.".

[8]Cf. Acts 19:40.

Purpose

Because of their acceptance of the message which Paul preached, and the evident change in their way of life, the Thessalonians had become the object of Jewish persecution. To those who were thus beset by afflictions, Paul wrote this Epistle as a message of comfort and encouragement. He rejoiced that they were standing firm and he himself was comforted by the news which Timothy had brought to him at Corinth (3:1-10).

In addition it would appear that he wrote in lieu of another visit (2:17, 18). Satan had "hindered"[9] them, and so the desired reunion had to be postponed.

Finally, there was the matter of doctrine. Some erroneous ideas concerning the coming of Christ apparently had arisen, and Paul writes to correct them. It should be noted that this is the chief theme of the Epistle. The mention of it occurs at the end of every chapter (see 1:10; 2:19; 3:13; 4:13-17; 5:23). Besides, 5:1-10 sketches the nature of the Day of the Lord and the need for vigilance in view of it.

Outline

I. Salutation   1:1

II. Thanksgiving   1:2-10

III. The Pauline Ministry Defended   2:1—3:13
   1. Vindication of his message   2:1-12
   2. Commendation on their progress   2:13-20
   3. Appreciation of their endurance   3:1-13

IV. The Christian Walk Delineated   4:1-5:24
   1. Exhortation to do the will of God   4:1-12
   2. Expectation of the coming of Christ   4:13-18
   3. Application to the life of the believer   5:1-24

V. Conclusion   5:25-28

---

[9]The verb occurs in only four other places in the New Testament (see Acts 24:4; Rom. 15:22; Gal. 5:7; I Peter 3:7). The Romans passage is very similar to the one under discussion. While Paul does not say *how* Satan hindered him, passages like Job 1:6-12; Zechariah 3:1 and Daniel 10:12, 13 show the reality of his power. Cf. W. Hendriksen, *I and II Thessalonians* in his *New Testament Commentary* (Grand Rapids: Baker Book House, 1955), pp. 75, 76; G. Milligan, *op. cit.*, p. 34.

Silas (cf. Acts 15:27, 32, 40) and Timothy (cf. Acts 16: 1-3) joined with Paul in sending greetings to the Church in Thessalonica. They acknowledge with true thankfulness the influence of this congregation. Having become "imitators"[10] of the apostles, and of the Lord (1:6), they became an "ensample"[11] to all the believers in Macedonia and Achaia, and from Thessalonica the word of the Lord spread far and wide (1:7, 8). Paul recalls for them how they 1) turned to God from idols, 2) to serve a living and true God, and 3) to wait for His Son from Heaven (1:9, 10).

Chapters two and three are primarily concerned with Paul's own ministry. Because God has entrusted him with the Gospel (2:4), his message is a valid one. Both by words and by works his ministry has been exemplary (2:10). He reminds them how they received his message at the first as "the word of God" (2:13) and lived in the light of that standard. The message which Timothy brought to him of their endurance in affliction was a great comfort (3:6-8).

Finally, Paul turns directly to the subject of the Christian life. God's will for the believer is his sanctification (4:3, 7) rather than a life of uncleanness. This life is to be lived in the light of the second coming of Christ, which is a source of comfort (4:13-18) and a challenge (5:1-11). This hope is to be so real that the ordinary affairs of life will be affected by it (5:12-24). The enumeration of specific duties in these verses covers both religious and moral obligations. Whether in public or personal relationships, the Christian has definite responsibilities toward God, toward his neighbors and brethren in the Lord, and toward himself. The consummation of this total picture will be a wholly sanctified individual at the coming of our Lord Jesus Christ (5:23). What is the guarantee of such a promise and the assurance of the believer's enablement to ful-

---

[10]The Greek term is the basis of our English word "mimics" (*mimētai*). (See also I Cor. 4:16; 11:1; Eph. 5:1; I Thess. 2:14; Heb. 6:12.)

[11]Literally, a "type" (*typos*), a "pattern" of the moral life. W. F. Arndt and F. W. Gingrich, *A Greek-English Lexicon of the New Testament and Other Early Christian Literature* (Chicago: University of Chicago Press, 1956), p. 837. (See Titus 2:7; I Tim. 4:12; Phil. 3:17; II Thess. 3:9; I Peter 5:3.)

fill his tasks? It is given in this final word: "Faithful is he that calleth you, who also will do it" (5:24).

II THESSALONIANS

Author

The writer identifies himself by name in 1:1 and 3:17. In addition, the references to Paul's travels (1:10; 3:7-10), the attempts by some to usurp his authority (2:2) and the doctrinal and hortatory sections which are similar to I Thessalonians are in keeping with the statement of authorship. The external testimony, from the early second century, substantiates that of the book itself.

Date and Destination

While still at Corinth, and probably only a short time after the writing of the first Epistle, Paul wrote the second letter to Thessalonica.[12] The date, therefore, is probably A.D. 51, and the destination is the same as that of the former Epistle.

Purpose

From even a cursory reading of the Epistle, it is clear that Paul wrote to correct mistaken ideas concerning the Day of the Lord. Because someone had written a letter to the Church purporting to be from Paul (2:2), saying that the Day of the Lord had already come and that the period of tribulation was upon them, the believers were distressed. Before that day comes, said Paul, certain important events must occur (2:3-7), which evidently have not as yet happened. Others, feeling that the Lord's coming was imminent, had stopped working and were living in idleness (3:10, 11). An injunction concerning Christian industry and needed discipline is given to correct this false outlook.

Outline

The main theme of the Epistle revolves around "the day of

---

[12]G. T. Manley, ed., *The New Bible Handbook* (London: Inter-Varsity Fellowship, 1953), p. 380.

the Lord." Paul assures the saints (chap. 1), warns (chap. 2), and exhorts (chap. 3) in view of these coming events.

I. Salutation   1:1, 2

II. Anticipation of the Day of the Lord   1:3-12

III. Description of the Day of the Lord   2:1-17

IV. Exhortation to Prayer and Proper Conduct in
    View of the Day of the Lord   3:1-16

V. Conclusion   3:17, 18

Since Paul had left Thessalonica (cf. Acts 17:10), persecution had been the lot of the Church. The attacks which had been directed first against the apostle were turned toward the believers there. Because of their endurance under the pressure of these onslaughts, Paul gave thanks to God for them. The day was coming, he assured them, when the Lord Jesus would be revealed[13] from Heaven to take vengeance on all those "who know not God" (1:7, 8). The scene depicted here, one of judgment upon God's enemies, may be contrasted with that spoken of in I Thessalonians 4:13-17. The latter is a source of comfort to the believers as it promises that "we shall ever be with the Lord."[14]

Paul launches into the heart of his message at 2:1. Due to the false reports and rumors which were being circulated, the Thessalonians had become troubled concerning the time of "the day of the Lord" (2:2). The apostle makes it clear that this part of God's program could not be fulfilled until the great apostasy and the appearance of the Man of Sin (2:3). As he had not yet been revealed, the Day of the Lord was yet future. When he appeared, the Lord Jesus would "slay [him] with the breath of his mouth" (2:8). One further event which was

---

[13]Cf. Luke 17:30, where Jesus refers to "the day that the Son of man is revealed." G. Milligan, op. cit., pp. 145-151, differentiates between the Greek terms translated "presence" (parousia), "manifestation" (epiphaneia) and "revelation" (apocalypsis). See also W. Hendriksen, op. cit., p. 158 and footnote 115.

[14]See H. B. Swete, The Appearances of Our Lord After the Passion (London: Macmillan and Co., Ltd., 1908), pp. 141-149.

to herald this period was the removal of "the restrainer" (2:6, 7), which would allow evil to break out in fury. Who or what this "restrainer" was is difficult to determine at this point in time.[15]

The final injunctions (chap. 3) enlarge on the exhortations of I Thessalonians 4:9-12. Paul here gives his remedy for idleness: "If any will not work, neither let them eat" (3:10). Surely the implied alternative would eventually bring about a renewal of industry!

Suggested Readings

BACKGROUND

Conybeare, W. J. and Howson, J. S. *The Life and Epistles of St. Paul.* London: Longmans, Green, and Co., 1898. (U.S. publisher: Eerdmans, 1949.) Old but valuable study.

Fairweather, W. *The Background of the Epistles.* Edinburgh: T. & T. Clark, 1935. The historical, literary, religious and doctrinal backgrounds of the New Testament letters.

Hayes, D. A. *Paul and His Epistles.* N. Y.: The Methodist Book Concern, 1915. Thorough introduction to the life and writings of Paul. Good bibliography of older works in the field.

Hiebert, D. E. *An Introduction to the Pauline Epistles.* Chicago: Moody Press, 1954. Contains annotated bibliography after each epistle. Among the best books in this field.

Machen, J. G. *The Origin of Paul's Religion.* Grand Rapids: Wm. B. Eerdmans Publishing Co., 1947.

Ridderbos, H. *Paul and Jesus.* Translated by D. H. Freeman. Philadelphia: The Presbyterian and Reformed Publishing Company, 1958.

Smith, D. *The Life and Letters of St. Paul.* London: Hodder & Stoughton, 1919.

Stalker, J. *Life of St. Paul.* Grand Rapids: Zondervan Publishing House, n.d. A convenient handbook for Bible class study.

---

[15]A brief summary of five suggested interpretations is given by C. F. Hogg and W. E. Vine, *The Epistles to the Thessalonians* (London: Pickering & Inglis, Ltd., 1959 edition), pp. 258-261. They are 1) Seneca, the tutor of Nero (the man of sin); 2) the Holy Spirit by the Church; 3) God, by His providence; 4) the Roman Empire and policy, together with the Emperors and their representatives; 5) Gentile dominion (i.e., constituted government) as referred to in such passages as Daniel 2:37-44; Luke 21:24; Romans 13:1-7; I Peter 2:13-17.

COMMENTARIES

Hendriksen, W. *Exposition of I and II Thessalonians* in *New Testament Commentary*. Grand Rapids: Baker Book House, 1955.

Hogg, C. F. and Vine, W. E. *The Epistles to the Thessalonians with Notes Exegetical and Expository*. Revised edition. London: Pickering & Inglis, Ltd., 1959.

Milligan, G. *St. Paul's Epistles to the Thessalonians*. London: Macmillan and Company, Ltd., 1908. (U.S. publisher: Eerdmans, 1952.) Advanced commentary on the Greek text.

Morris, L. *Commentary on the Epistles to the Thessalonians* in *The New International Commentary on the New Testament*. Grand Rapids: Wm. B. Eerdmans Publishing Co., 1959.

CHAPTER 10

THE PAULINE EPISTLES:
SOTERIOLOGICAL

Introduction

THESE FOUR EPISTLES, I and II Corinthians, Galatians and Romans, emphasize the doctrine of salvation. Although Galatians may have been written earlier than the others, it is included here because of the close doctrinal affinity which is evident among them. (See section on Galatians for details of date.)

The question of authorship of the four letters need not be raised. From earliest times the external testimony to Pauline authorship has been maintained, and even the radical Tübingen critics of the nineteenth century held that they were the genuine core of the apostle's correspondence. The Epistles themselves bear many marks of Paul's hand and all bear his name and the familiar greetings (cf. I Cor. 1:1-3; 16:21-24; II Cor. 1:1, 2; 10:1; Gal. 1:1-3; Rom. 1:1-7).

I CORINTHIANS

Among the soteriological epistles of Paul, I Corinthians is notable for its insistence that the cross of Christ is the instrument of sanctification, and is the basic solution to the moral issues of life. While Romans and Galatians emphasize the truth of justification by faith in Christ, I Corinthians was written to remind the believers that though they once had been spiritually and morally bankrupt, now they were "washed, sanctified and justified" (6:11), and that whether they ate or drank or whatsoever they did, they were to "do all to the glory of God" (10:31).

Within the Epistle itself, three main emphases may be discerned:

1. The evils of the partisan spirit (see esp. chaps. 1-4)
2. The Christian conscience (see esp. chaps. 8-10)
3. The power of the cross in salvation and sanctification.

The third of these major themes is applied to a number of specific matters, such as sexual propriety (5:1-13; 6:12-20), litigation (6:1-11), marriage (7:1-40), and conduct in the Church, including the use of spiritual gifts (11:1—14:40).

Date and Destination

Paul visited Corinth on his second missionary journey (Acts 18:1-17) and, with the sole exception of the Ephesian stay (Acts 19), spent more time in this city than any other place in the course of his missionary labors. His place of residence here was the home of Aquila and Priscilla and along with them he made tents to earn necessary funds. For over eighteen months he remained, "teaching the word of God among them" (Acts 18:11).

While Paul was in Corinth, Gallio, brother of Seneca the philosopher, was appointed as proconsul of the province of Achaia. As Corinth was the capital of the region, Gallio's residence was in this city. The date of his accession to the proconsularship was probably either A.D. 51 (Deissmann) or A.D. 52 (Ramsay). The Jews, outraged by Paul's preaching, brought him before Gallio, charging him with persuading the people "to worship God contrary to the law" (Acts 18:13). Luke recounts that Gallio, seeing that it was a Jewish and not a Roman dispute, "cared for none of these things" (Acts 18:17). His indifference was a boon to Paul.

Leaving Corinth, Paul returned to Antioch, then set out on his third journey, coming shortly to Ephesus (Acts 19:1). While here, in the mid-fifties, he wrote the First Epistle to the Corinthians (I Cor. 16:8). The Epistle may therefore be dated at about A.D. 55.

Destroyed in 146 B.C. by the Roman general Mummius, and rebuilt in 46 B.C. by Julius Caesar, Corinth in the first century of our era was a large, prosperous, cosmopolitan city and the capital of Achaia. Along with cities like Antioch of Pisidia and

Philippi, Corinth was classed as a Roman colony. Being one of the leading commercial cities of the Mediterranean, she attracted people of every kind, class and nationality. Her reputation was not desirable because of widespread immorality. To call one "a Corinthian" was to use a slang expression for the vilest kind of person. The poor and the wealthy, the wise and the ignorant, beauty and ugliness stood side by side in Corinth. Paul's words in the Epistle reflect something of these conditions (see esp. 1:18-31; 5:1; 6:9, 10, 15-18; 8:4).

Amid these conditions, the Gospel of Christ had made its impact. People had been converted (Acts 18:8-10; I Cor. 6: 11) and a Church had been formed (I Cor. 1:2). The Epistle is directed toward its members who found themselves beset "without and within" with vexing problems which struck at the heart of their Christian experience.

Purpose

The occasion for the writing of the Epistle was twofold: Paul had received reports from the family of Chloe (1:11) of serious problems in the Corinthian Church; he had also had a letter from the Corinthians themselves (7:1) filled with questions which perplexed them.

With a view to advising them and correcting these serious aberrations, Paul writes this Epistle and deals at length with many of the issues involved. His constant theme is that the cross of Christ and His Lordship must dominate in every area of individual and corporate living. It is truly a presentation of the doctrine of sanctification in its broadest aspects. Though the style is informal, the Epistle is freighted with the voice of authority.

Outline

The general theme of I Corinthians may be discerned in Paul's plea for *Christian unity*. That unity which is spoken of is not primarily doctrinal. Only chapter fifteen deals directly with a doctrine—that of the resurrection. But it is first of all a unity of mind (cf. 2:16) which will bring about a corresponding oneness in living (cf. 10:31).

I. Introduction   1:1-9
   Salutation   1:1-3
   Thanksgiving   1:4-9

II. Reply to Reports from Chloe   1:10—6:20
   1. The problem of divisions   1:10—4:21
   2. The problem of sexual immorality   5:1-13
   3. The problem of litigation   6:1-11
   4. The problem of defilement   6:12-20

III. Reply to the Letter from Corinth   7:1—16:9
   1. The problem of marriage   7:1-41
   2. The problem of conscience   8:1—10:33
   3. The problem of conduct in the church   11:1-34
   4. The problem of spiritual gifts   12:1-14:39
   5. The problem of the resurrection   15:1-58
   6. The problem of giving   16:1-9

IV. Conclusion   16:10-24

In view of the apparent conditions in the Corinthian Church, the introduction to the Epistle is striking. One of the reasons for which Paul thanks God for these people is that they "come behind in no gift" (1:7). They had been the recipients of rich spiritual blessings (1:5). Further, the apostle states that God would confirm them "unto the end" (1:9). These statements, relating to the spiritual endowments of the Corinthian believers, are in vivid contrast to what follows in the remainder of the Epistle. Those who are called "saints" (1:2) need to live in accordance with their position in Christ.

A relatively large amount of text is devoted to the problem of divisions or schisms (1:10). The issue revolved around favoritism toward certain outstanding persons. Some championed Paul, the great exponent of Christian liberty and the spiritual father of the Corinthian Church. Others favored Apollos, the leading orator of the early Church and a man "mighty in the scriptures" (Acts 18:24). A third favorite was Cephas (Peter), first leader of the Jerusalem Church and champion of strict orthodoxy. Finally, a fourth group, with a naïve and superior air, said they were simply "of Christ." It is felt that the fourth attitude was the most dangerous and reprehensible of all, as it intimated that Christ was the special property of a select few.[1]

Such ideas were potentially fatal to the unity of the group and Paul severely rebukes them. The burden of these first four chapters is that God is sovereign among His people, the apostles are simply His servants, and spiritual prosperity and Christian unity are possible only in the acknowledgment of these truths. Further, the life of each believer will one day be scrutinized, tried by fire (3:13), and the way in which one has "built upon the foundation" (3:12) will be the basis for reward or loss.

The remaining chapters (5, 6) are concerned basically with the questions of moral purity and litigation. When Paul receives the report of the case of incest, he censures the church for their failure to administer discipline and pronounces severe judgment on the individual concerned (5:1 ff.). His decision "to deliver such a one unto Satan for the destruction of the flesh, that the spirit may be saved in the day of the Lord Jesus" (5:5), is one of the most drastic pronouncements in the New Testament.[2] Following the censure of the practice of taking lawsuits before heathen courts (6:1-11), Paul emphasizes the necessity for realizing that the believer's body is 1) for the Lord (6:13), 2) a member of Christ (6:15), and 3) a temple of the Holy Spirit (6:19). The gross immorality of Corinth necessitated stringent reminders of these truths.[3]

In the second major division of the Epistle Paul deals with

[1]P. Schaff, *History of the Apostolic Church* (New York: Charles Scribner, 1867), pp. 285-291, has an extended discussion of the situation existing in Corinth. A. Robertson and A. Plummer, *A Critical and Exegetical Commentary on the First Epistle of St. Paul to the Corinthians* (Edinburgh: T. & T. Clark, 1953), pp. 11-13, state, "To say, with special emphasis, 'I am of Christ,' is virtually to say that Christ is mine and not yours."

[2]Robertson and Plummer, *ibid.*, p. 99, accept both interpretations of the passage: (1) that which sees here the destruction of "sinful lusts" (cf. I Tim. 1:20 and the Pauline use of "flesh" in Rom. 8:13 and Col. 3:5); (2) that view which includes physical suffering (cf. I Cor. 11:30; Acts 5:1, f; 13:11). It should be noted, too, that the punishment here is remedial, as also in I Timothy 1:20.

[3]P. Schaff, *History of the Christian Church* (New York: Charles Scribner's Sons, 1884), Vol I, p. 758, footnote 1.

questions contained in a letter sent to him from Corinth (see 7:1; 7:25; 8:1; 11:2; 12:1; 15:1; 16:1). They are varied in nature, reflecting the complexity of conditions in the nascent Church. Domestic, social, ecclesiastical, doctrinal and economic problems are discussed in these chapters.

The section on marriage (chap. 7) has to do with two extremes, the tendency to immorality and the opposite state, celibacy or asceticism. It hardly seems fair, on the basis of this chapter alone, to say that Paul was opposed to marriage. His use of the marriage relationship in Ephesians 5:22-32 as an illustration of the union of Christ and the Church would seem to invalidate such a position. Probably a more basic approach is to notice his emphasis in verses 7 and 24 which stresses each individual is to recognize his gift from God and live his life accordingly. Within the marriage bond there is the necessity of unity of spirit and unselfishness of motive, the latter being emphasized in the case of a believer and an unbeliever.

Another problem, one which has extended through the ages in principle at least, is that of matters of conscience (chaps. 8-10). To what extent may a Christian exercise his "rights"? What effect do the scruples of others have upon my way of life? Am I free "to do as I please"? Paul cites a number of specific illustrations,[4] but ends with a general principle which covers every area of life (10:31). This standard, "the glory of God," is not something new with Paul. The Lord Jesus had spoken of it to His disciples in an earlier day. "Even so let your light shine before men; that they may see your good works, and glorify your Father who is in heaven" (Matt. 5:16). Our basic motivation is not to be a selfish one; the "first and greatest commandment" is to love God, then to love our neighbor as ourselves.

As has been noted earlier, Corinth was not famed for morality. Two evidences of this were dealt with in chapter eleven: the conduct of women in the Church and disorders at the Lord's Table. In view of their newfound freedom, some of the women

---

[4]The eating of meat offered to idols (8:1, 4, 13), the financial dependence of the minister upon those to whom he ministers (9:11-14), and socializing with unbelievers (10:27) are all examples of particular situations which raised questions in the minds of some in Corinth.

were throwing off restraints which had formerly bound them. They were going about in public without their customary veiling. As a sign of your subjection, says Paul, you must be veiled (11:5, ff.). It is, moreover, dishonoring to God to cast away proper dress.[5]

Furthermore, the observance of the Lord's Supper was being turned into a shameful orgy of eating and drinking. It was preceded by the *Agape,* the common fellowship meal, at which some of the members of the Church were overindulging themselves. When they came to the communion service, they were physically, mentally and spiritually unfit for such an observance. For this reason, says Paul, God has judged you and so "many among you are weak and sickly, and not a few sleep" (I Cor. 11:30). The apostle gives sober advice to the Corinthians as he says, "Let a man prove himself, and so let him eat of the bread and drink of the cup" (11:28).

A large part of the Epistle is concerned with the problem of the use and abuse of spiritual gifts. Paul makes several points very clear as he deals with this situation: 1) the gifts are manifestations of the Holy Spirit in the believer (12:4-11); 2) they are to be exercised in a spirit of love (13:1-13); 3) things are to be done "decently and in order" (14:40). The sovereignty of God in the Church is emphasized in this passage. He has placed the members in the Body "even as it pleased him" (12:18), and each member is subject to Him as well as to every other member. Only as the members serve in this way can the Body be assured of proper operation. Strife, jealousy and envy will not advance but only deter the well-being of the whole organism. Again the plea for unity is evident.

The only purely doctrinal issue in the Epistle is dealt with in chapter 15. "How say some among you that there is no resurrection from the dead?" (15:12).[6] In expounding on this pri-

---

[5]"If, argues the Apostle, you will cast off your veil, go all the way: cut off your hair, and proclaim yourself a widow; shave your head, and proclaim yourself an adulteress." David Smith, *The Life and Letters of St. Paul* (London: Hodder & Stoughton, 1919), p. 283.
[6]This key doctrine was frequently dealt with by Paul in the face of denials by various persons. In Acts 17, the apostle proclaimed this truth to the Athenian Stoics and Epicureans, both of whom denied the idea. There

mary doctrine of the faith, Paul states first the historical basis of the resurrection: Christ has risen (15:1-11). Second, the meaning of the resurrection is declared (15:12-57). Because Christ has risen, all men shall rise from the dead. The Christian is to have a new body (15:42-49) and "shall inherit the kingdom of God" (15:50) in which God shall be "all in all" (15: 28).

The final problem is that of finance, the collection for the poor in the Jerusalem church. Paul enunciates some basic principles for Christian giving. It should be regular, voluntary and proportionate (16:2).

Throughout the Epistle, in the face of the difficult questions with which he was confronted, Paul has maintained his plea for Christian unity. The cross of Christ needs to be applied to every area of life. Tenney has succinctly summarized the Epistle as follows:[7]

> Each problem was met by applying a spiritual principle rather than by recommending a psychological expedient. For schism, the remedy is spiritual maturity (3:1-9); for fornication, church discipline until the offender repents and is restored (5:1-5); for litigation there should be arbitration within the Christian community (6:1-6). In the case of marriage between a believer and an unbeliever, the concern of the believer is to save the unbeliever, not to alienate him or her (7:16); for the problem of the unmarried virgins, self-control or lawful marriage (7:36, 37). In the casuistic questions of food offered to idols and of details of worship, the relation of the believer to God is the deciding factor (10:31; 11:13, 32). Similarly the gifts are administered by God (12:28) within the church.

"The Lost Letter to Corinth"

A special note should be appended here concerning the so-called "lost letter." In I Corinthians 5:9, Paul writes, "I wrote

were in Ephesus men in the Church who taught "that the resurrection was past already" and were undermining the faith of some (II Tim. 2:17). (See also Acts 23:6; 24:15, 21; 26:8; Rom. 1:4; 6:5; Phil. 3:10, 11; and [one of the classic passages on the subject] especially I Thess. 4:13-18.)

[7]M. C. Tenney, *The New Testament: An Historical and Analytic Survey* (Grand Rapids: Eerdmans, 1953), p. 311.

unto you in my epistle to have no company with fornicators."
Apparently the letter has completely vanished. It seems to have
been written for the purpose of insisting on moral purity within
the Church. Because of the misunderstanding of what he had
written, Paul elaborates on his statement in I Corinthians 5:10-
13. David Smith has suggested that two fragments of the letter
survive in I Corinthians 6:12-20 and II Corinthians 6:14—
7:1.[8]

II CORINTHIANS

The Second Epistle to Corinth differs in a number of respects
from the first, but primarily in this, that it is mainly concerned
with problems confronting Paul. It is, therefore, of a more
personal nature.[9] This is especially evident in chapters 10-13.

Date and Destination

Paul left Ephesus shortly after writing the First Epistle to
Corinth.[10] Acts 20 relates his journey to Macedonia before going to Achaia once again. II Corinthians 2:12, 13 adds a
further detail to the itinerary, namely, that Paul went through
Troas. Here he expected to meet Titus and to receive his report of conditions at Corinth. Being disappointed when Titus
did not appear. Paul went into Macedonia, and from this
place (probably Philippi) wrote the second Epistle (7:5-16).[11]

---

[9]*Op. cit.*, pp. 235-238 and p. 654. Tenney, however, says, "The hypothesis
rests solely on subjective impression; and however plausible it may seem,
there is no good external evidence to support it," *op. cit.*, p. 308.

[9]D. A. Hayes, *Paul and His Epistles* (New York: Methodist Book Concern,
1919), pp. 258-260, calls II Corinthians "the most intensely personal"
and "the most emotional" of the Pauline Epistles.

[10]From II Corinthians 12:14 and 13:1, where Paul writes of coming to
them a "third time," it is possible to assume that during his stay in Ephesus
he made the brief trip across the Aegean Sea to Corinth in an attempt to
straighten out conditions in the Church. Apparently Timothy, sent to
Corinth with the first Epistle according to I Corinthians 16:10, 11 had not
been successful in this mission.

[11]In II Corinthians 2:4, Paul makes reference to a letter written "with
many tears." Whether this is a reference to I Corinthians, which seems
doubtful, or to another "lost epistle," is difficult to determine. A third suggestion has been made, namely, that this is a reference to II Corinthians
10 through 13 (which was later combined with chaps. 1–9). The first of
these views is allowed for by Manley (*The New Bible Handbook*, p. 362),
who refers to I Corinthians 3–6 as severe in tone. The second is accepted

Following shortly after I Corinthians, the letter may be dated about A.D. 56.

Purpose

W. Graham Scroggie[12] has made the suggestion that the second letter to Corinth reflects a division within the Corinthian Church, namely, a "majority group" which had repented of their erring ways (2:6, 7; 7:6, 7) and a "minority group" which still opposed Paul (10:10, "they say"). In the light of conditions at this point, then, Paul had a twofold purpose in penning this letter: 1) to express his thanks for the repentance of the many and 2) to answer the accusations of the few who discounted or denied the validity of his apostleship (11:5, 13, 23).[13]

Outline

The chief emphasis of II Corinthians is Paul's defense or vindication of his ministry and authority.

I. Salutation   1:1, 2

II. Problems of the Christian Ministry   1:3—7:16
    1. Details of personal relationships
    2. Declaration of the message

---

by H. C. Thiessen, *Introduction to the New Testament* (Grand Rapids: William B. Eerdmans, 1948), pp. 209, 210, who asks, "Could Paul have rightly regretted composing and sending a letter that he had written by inspiration?" The third is accepted by Scott as "the most satisfactory solution of a problem which undoubtedly exists." *The Literature of the New Testament* (New York: Morningside Heights: Columbia University Press, 1938), pp. 129, 130, 140-142, and by a number of other scholars. The consistent testimony of manuscript evidence, however, is against this view.

---

[12]*The New Testament* in *Know Your Bible*, Vol. II (London: Pickering & Inglis, Ltd., 1950), pp. 136-139. Rather than dividing the composition of the letter into two parts (1-9, 10-13) as some have done, Scroggie believes that the two sections of the single letter were directed toward two respective groups.

[13]Compare the similar problem which Paul faced in Galatia. His authority and his message were being undermined by the Judaizers and he defends both by appealing to his conversion, his commission from Christ and his subsequent experiences (Gal. 1:1, 12-24; 2:1-10, 16, 21).

III. Problems of Christian Giving   8:1—9:15
     1. A willing spirit
     2. A cheerful disposition

IV. Problems of a Christian Minister   10:1—13:10
     1. Vindication of apostleship
     2. Edification and reproof

V. Conclusion   13:11-14

As Paul begins to write this letter to Corinth, he is conscious of the divine purpose in the midst of affliction. Whether his own personal circumstances are considered (1:8-11), or the problems in the Corinthian Church (2:5-11), the basic answer applies: God comforts us; we are thereby strengthened; we, in turn, are able to comfort others (1:4). Even as the Epistle ends, the prayer and desire of the apostle is that they "be perfected" (13:11).[14]

Accompanying this note is that of "thanksgiving" to God. This term occurs in rather striking places. In 2:14, it is thanks to God for triumph in the ministry of the Gospel; in 8:16, for the earnest care of Titus for the Corinthian Church; in 9:15, for God's "unspeakable gift."[15]

The first major section of the letter is divided largely between personal matters (cf. 1:3—2:13; 6:11—7:16) and a defense of the message which Paul preached (cf. 2:14—6:10). The two, however, are to a degree intertwined and not easily separated. As was noted above, this epistle is highly personal throughout. One common emphasis of this entire section is the work of God on behalf of believers. God comforts (1:3, 4;

---

[14]The verb translated "perfected" is a graphic one. It first occurs in the New Testament in Matthew 4:21 (cf. Mark 1:19). James and John, who were fishermen, were "mending their nets." The Greek physician Galen used the noun form to describe "the setting of a bone." Arndt and Gingrich, *A Greek-English Lexicon of the New Testament and Other Early Christian Literature* (Chicago: University of Chicago Press, 1956), p. 418, render II Corinthians 13:11 as "mend your ways." (See also Gal. 6:1; I Cor. 1:10; I Thess. 3:10; I Peter 5:10.)

[15]Paul seemingly has reference to the giving of the Son (cf. John 3:16), and means to say, "If God gave such a great gift that words cannot describe it, surely you should be willing to give of your material means to help those in need." (Cf. I Cor. 15:57, where Paul "thanks" God for victory over death through the resurrection.)

7:6), delivers (1:10), establishes (1:21, 22), gives victory
(2:14), enables (3:6), enlightens (4:6), empowers (4:7),
resurrects (4:14), prepares (5:5), reconciles (5:18), be-
seeches (5:20) and receives as a Father (6:17, 18).

By citing the example of the liberality of the Churches of
Macedonia (Philippi, Thessalonica, Berea), Paul exhorts the
Corinthian saints to fulfill that which they had promised to do
a year before (8:10, 11). Titus had been sent by Paul to su-
pervise a collection of money for the benefit of the needy saints
in Jerusalem. Because they had delayed in giving of their material goods, Paul wrote this eloquent reminder setting forth the
principles of Christian giving. "Thus we learn from the Scriptures that we have a duty towards our poorer brethren in the
Lord; and that the fulfillment of this duty can have rich spiritual
significance."[16]

A vigorous defense of his apostleship is contained in the last
part of the Epistle (10:1—13:10) together with some basic
exhortations and words of reproof. It seems likely that a group
in Corinth was opposed to Paul's authority. Notice the following expressions in these chapters: "some" (10:2); "any man"
(10:7); "they say" (10:10); "such a one" (10:11), "certain
of them" (10:12); "such men" (11:13). The apostle therefore
recounts his appointment by the Lord (10:8; 13:10), his apostolic labors and sufferings as a minister of Christ (11:23-31),
his "visions and revelations of the Lord" (12:1-9), and the
"signs of an apostle" which they had seen during his stay in
Corinth (12:11-13). All these are designed to be evidences
of the genuineness of his authority and his message.

The final words of benediction are unique in the writings of
the New Testament. They are fuller than Paul's usual benedic-
tions and embrace the Persons of the Trinity: "The grace of the
Lord Jesus Christ, and the love of God, and the communion of
the Holy Spirit, be with you all" (13:14).

[16]W. C. G. Proctor, *The Epistles to the Corinthians* in *The New Bible
Commentary* (Grand Rapids: Wm. B. Eerdmans, 1956), p. 995. For the
same thought see I John 3:16-18; I Corinthians 16:1-4.

No letter of the New Testament outranks Galatians in historical and theological importance. Although it is brief, it has, from the time of writing, held a vital place in the life of the Church. Three reasons for its prominence have been suggested: 1) Historically, it gives an early account of the nascent Christian Church; 2) Theologically, Galatians is the main key showing Paul's interpretation of the Christian message; 3) Religiously, the book retains abiding value as the Christian declaration of true spiritual liberty.[17]

Date and Destination

The Epistle has been dated from 48/49 to 57/58. If the early date is assigned, the writing would precede the Jerusalem Council (A.D. 49/50) and would rank Galatians as the earliest of Paul's Epistles and second only in time to the Epistle of James. Ramsay placed Galatians in the early fifties, while Lightfoot assigned it to the later period suggested above. The question of dating is partially dependent on a larger problem, namely, the destination of the book.

Galatia originally was an area in the northeastern part of Asia Minor. It had been settled by invading Gauls from northern Europe in the third century B.C. When the Romans subjugated the land in 25 B.C. they reorganized the territory, incorporating an area to the south of the Gallic region, and named the whole new province Galatia. In the first century of the Christian era, therefore, the term might be used of the old territory (ethnic Galatia) or the new (provincial Galatia).[18]

Most older commentators (such as Lightfoot and Conybeare and Howson) defended the North Galatian theory. As Paul could not have gone into this area until his second journey (Acts 16), the Epistle accordingly would have to be dated later. Since the time of Sir William Ramsay many scholars have adopted the so-called South Galatian theory (see Tenney, Rid-

---

[17]E. F. Scott, op. cit., pp. 145, 146.
[18]The chief cities of old or north Galatia were Ancyra, Pessinus and Tavium. In Acts 13, 14, the cities of south Galatia are Antioch (of Pisidia), Iconium, Lystra and Derbe.

derbos). This view would see the letter sent to the cities of Acts 13, 14, and would also allow for an earlier dating.

A more basic issue than the date alone is the matter of the main issue at stake in Galatians, the controversy centering around the question of law and grace as related to salvation. This was the problem dealt with by the Jerusalem Council (Acts 15). It seems strange that if Paul wrote the Epistle following the Council (after A.D. 50) that he would not call upon that historic decision to settle the problem of legalism in Galatia. In his controversy with Peter regarding matters of conduct (2:11, ff.) Paul rather appeals to the logical basis of the Gospel (see esp. 2:16). When addressing the Galatians on the questions of justification and sanctification, his appeals are to experience and the Scriptures. Once the Council had rendered its decision, a strong weapon would be at hand in settling a dispute of this kind.

Other elements, such as the possibility that the Galatians were acquainted with Barnabas (2:1, 9, 13), Paul's companion on the first journey only (Acts 13, 14), the fact that the main Roman roads ran through the cities of South Galatia, and the presence of the Judaizers in this area,[19] point toward the destination of the letter as the churches of Antioch, Iconium, Lystra and Derbe.

If this be the proper conclusion as to destination, much is known of Paul's work in the Galatian Churches. Acts 13 and 14 give a detailed account of the apostle's experiences in the founding and establishing of these congregations. His notable address in the synagogue at Antioch of Pisidia concludes on a note that epitomizes the message of the Galatian Epistle (13: 38, 39). The welcome accorded him at Lystra (14:11 ff.) may well be reflected in the Epistle (4:14). In Acts 16:1-5 Luke records Paul's return to this territory where he adds young Timothy to the missionary party.

Purpose

Galatians is a polemic against the idea that a man can be

---

[19]There were very few Jews in the cities of North Galatia, according to Ramsay, while many were to be found in the southern area.

justified by works. The occasion for the letter was the shocking news which came to Paul (1:6, 7) that the Galatian Churches were being infested by legalists who preached "a different gospel" which was not "good news" at all. The apostle's purpose, therefore, in penning this letter was to establish in the minds of his converts the true Gospel—that "a man is not justified by the works of the law, but by faith in Jesus Christ" (2:16). In solemn language he pronounces an anathema on any and all who preach any other Gospel. The call to maintain the freedom which they have gained in Christ is sounded particularly in 5:1, 13.

Outline

Due to its logical arrangement, Galatians is easily outlined. Based on the central theme of justification by faith (2:16) the following analysis emerges:

I. Introduction   1:1-10
   1. Salutation   1:1-5
   2. Occasion for writing   1:6-10
II. The Autobiographical Argument:
    the Gospel Revealed   1:11—2:21
   1. Direct revelation of the Gospel   1:11-24
   2. Apostolic confirmation of the Gospel   2:1-10
   3. Personal application of the Gospel   2:11-21
III. The Doctrinal Argument: the Gospel
    Prophesied   3:1—4:31
   1. The personal appeal   3:1-5
   2. The experience of Abraham   3:6-14
   3. The promise and the law   3:15-22
   4. The nature of sonship   3:23—4:7
   5. The danger of defection   4:8-20
   6. The lesson by allegory   4:21-31
IV. The Practical Argument: the Gospel
    Applied   5:1—6:10
   1. The call to live in freedom   5:1-15
   2. The contrast of flesh and Spirit   5:16-24
   3. The challenge to walk by the Spirit   5:25—6:10
V. Conclusion   6:11-18

With a specific declaration of his apostleship and without any word of commendation, Paul addresses the churches of Galatia. His tone is severe due to the issue at stake. The message that Christ has "delivered us" is being undermined by "another [kind of] gospel," and Paul with powerful strokes sets out to defend the true evangel.

By means of a threefold attack he presents his case. First, he relates his own experience; second, he demonstrates that the Gospel has its roots in the Old Testament; third, that this message is the true answer to the problem of life.

What is the source of this message that Paul preaches? Human, say his opponents; divine, says Paul. Drawing upon his own background as a rabbinical student, he makes it clear that he did not receive it from man, nor was he taught it, but that his Gospel was "by revelation of Jesus Christ" (1:12). Further, this message was confirmed by the leaders of the Jerusalem Church, Peter, James[20] and John, who gave to Paul "the right hand of fellowship (Gal. 2:9). Finally, this message was one that Paul himself had experienced and of which he was a convinced proponent.[21] The basis of Paul's rebuke of Peter (2:11 ff.) at Antioch was that justification came by faith in Christ and was not gained by the observance of a certain standard of life. The new way of life, however, was to grow out of the experience of identification with Christ (2:20).

Having set forth the argument from his own life, Paul turns to the Scriptures and appeals to their witness to substantiate his case further. By means of a series of questions, the answers to which are quite evident (3:1-5), the apostle seeks to arouse the Galatians from their spiritual confusion. Has someone cast the evil eye upon them? Have they forgotten that they received

---

[20]James, "the Lord's brother" (1:19), not the brother of John, one of the original Twelve whom Herod Agrippa I had killed (Acts 12). The man appearing in this passage was an unbeliever during the earthly life of Christ (John 7:5). Jesus appeared to him after the resurrection (I Cor. 15:7); he is found in the prayer meeting in Jerusalem (Acts 1:14), then appears in Acts 12, 15 and 21 as leader of the Jerusalem church.

[21]The Gospel is both objective (1:12) and subjective (2:16). It had come from an outside source, but it had also arrested Paul and become a part of him.

the Holy Spirit by faith at the first? Do they expect, therefore, to come to maturity by the works of the law rather than by that same Spirit? What does the Scripture have to say? Plainly this, that "Abraham believed God, and it was counted to him for righteousness," that is, he was justified (3:6).

Not only this, but Abraham received the promise long before the law was given. The law, furthermore, was given only to magnify transgressions and to lead one to Christ (3:19, 24). In two respects, then, promise excels law: in time and in purpose. Those who enter into this new relationship with Christ are described as "sons" in the family of God. Sonship, by nature, is superior to the state of immaturity ("children") under law.

One of the classic statements of the nature and meaning of redemption is to be found in 4:4-7. Paul, elaborating on the phrase, "But in the fullness of the time, God sent forth his Son" (4:4) sets forth 1) the *preparation for* and 2) the *purpose of* the coming of Christ. The first of these has been sketched in some detail in chapter one (see page 7, ff.). The second may be analyzed as follows: 1) the redemption of sinners (v. 5), 2) the adoption of sons (v. 5), 3) the mission of the Spirit (v. 6).

After warning the Galatians of the danger of their current defection (4:8-20), Paul pens a final illustration of the antithetical nature of law and promise. The story of the two sons of Abraham, Ishmael and Isaac, provides a picture of the principle that law and grace cannot exist together as the basis of justification (4:21-31).

Finally, the apostle employs the practical argument. He appeals to the sense of freedom in the lives of the Galatians. By the use of contrasting figures he shows the superiority of life in the Spirit to bondage under the law. Believers are exhorted to "stand fast" in their freedom, and to give expression to the new life in Christ by showing forth "the fruit of the Spirit."

Paul shows clearly the alternatives. Those "who would be justified by the law," he states, "are fallen away from grace" (5:4). If one seeks to establish his own righteousness, Christ is of no profit to him; His death was a meaningless gesture. The logical consequence of such an attitude is that the individual should place himself under the whole law and, as a debtor, observe it fully.

What, then, is the secret of victory? How can one be free from the bondage of the condemnation of God's law? The flesh (the old nature) within the believer demands its rights. It, being contrary to God, continually brings one into further bondage. Paul clearly gives the answer: "Walk by the Spirit, and ye will not fulfill the works of the flesh" (5:16). True freedom is not manifested by producing "the works of the flesh" (5:19-21) but by bearing "the fruit of the Spirit" (5: 22, 23). This is what it means to be "a spiritual Christian."

These are no meaningless platitudes. The principle here enshrined has its logical expression in specific acts of kindness (6:1-10). Has a brother fallen? Lift him up. Does one bear a crushing burden? Help him by sharing his load. Is one in need? Aid him. This is the result of the application of the Gospel to the daily life of the believer.

Paul's conclusion to the Epistle (6:11-18) is most fitting. He stresses again his concern for the Gospel he preaches and his personal involvement in the message. His dedication to the task speaks for itself (6:14, 17) and his hope is that once and for all the issue is clear and the controversy concluded.

ROMANS

While this Epistle is not chronologically prior to Paul's other writings, its primary place in the printed text of the Bible is not accidental. As a basic treatment of the subject of redemption it is foundational to the rest of the truths of God's revelation. Romans begins where man is by nature, showing him to be lost and undone. Then it leads logically through a discussion of condemnation, justification, and sanctification.

Date and Destination

After leaving Ephesus and traveling through Macedonia on his third journey, the apostle came again to Corinth (Acts 19:

21; 20:2, 3; Rom. 15:23-28). During his stay there he wrote to the Roman Church, in lieu of a personal visit, and seemingly sent the letter by the hand of the deaconess Phoebe (Rom. 16: 1, 2). The date of writing would therefore be about A.D. 55/ 56.

As to the origin of the Church in Rome, specific details are lacking. Among the major suggestions are (1) the work of Peter, (2) converts returning from Jerusalem following the day of Pentecost or 3) converts (probably Pauline) moving from various provinces of the Empire. In the light of the New Testament record itself, the first may be discounted. There is no positive evidence contained for this view in the New Testament, and it appears most unlikely that Paul would fail to address the leading apostle if he had been connected with that Church. While the second view remains a possible solution, the third has more to support it as chapter sixteen of the Epistle shows that Paul had many friends in Rome although he had not yet visited the city.[22]

Purpose

In the light of the statements found in 15:22-24, 29, 32, Paul hoped to visit Rome in the near future. Because there was uncertainty as to conditions in Jerusalem (15:31, 32), the letter was sent at this point.

Romans is a logical and comprehensive treatment of the basic truths of the Gospel. It may be that the Roman Church, because it had not had systematic apostolic teaching, needed such truth. Such an emphasis as is found in chapter thirteen, subjection to human rulers, would also be particularly applicable to Christians in the domain of Caesar.

Outline

The basic theme of Romans is *redemption*. Paul develops

---

[22]Some critics reject chapter sixteen as being a genuine part of the epistle. It may well be that the chapter was a part of the letter originally but that Paul sent the letter to other churches also and then omitted the last section as not being applicable. Priscilla and Aquila (Rom. 16:3, 4) had, before coming to Corinth (Acts 18:1) and Ephesus (I Cor. 16:19), resided in Rome (Acts 18:2).

the theme from five major points of view. The (key verses
are 1:16, 17.

I. Introduction   1:1-17
   1. Salutation   1:1-7
   2. Thanksgiving   1:8-15
   3. Theme   1:16, 17

II. Sin: the *Need* for Redemption   1:18—3:20
   1. Gentile sin   1:18—2:16
   2. Jewish sin   2:17—3:8
   3. Universal sin   3:9-20

III. Justification: the *Provision*
     of Redemption   3:21—5:21
   1. The fact   3:21-31
   2. The illustration   4:1-25
   3. The result   5:1-21

IV. Sanctification: the *Effect*
    of Redemption   6:1—8:39
   1. The union with Christ   6:1-23
   2. The conflict of natures   7:1-25
   3. The victory by the Spirit   8:1-39

V. Jew and Gentile: the *Scope*
   of Redemption   9:1—11:36
   1. Israel's past—God's judgment for sin   9:1-33
   2. Israel's present—God's offer of salvation   10:1-21
   3. Israel's future—God's promise
      of restoration   11:1-36

VI. Service: the *Fruit* of Redemption   12:1—15:13
   1. The call to dedication   12:1, 2
   2. The duties of life   12:3—13:14
   3. The principle of liberty   14:1—15:13

VII. Conclusion and Greetings   15:14—16:27

The Epistle unfolds in a series of successive steps showing the
logical nature of God's plan of redemption. By a style un-

matched in his other Epistles, Paul traces a person's spiritual progress from the lowest level of sin to the highest level of service.

Paul introduces himself to his Roman readers as one who has been commissioned and sent to deliver a message (an "apostle") and defines his message as the good news ("gospel") concerning God's Son, Jesus Christ. Together with thanksgiving to God for these fellow-believers, the writer crystallizes the message of the letter (1:16, 17) and launches into the main stream of thought.

Sin has brought about man's separation from God. It came about as a rejection of the knowledge of the Creator (1:18-20) and the end result was that "God gave them up" to their evil ways. Whether one views the condition of the heathen (idolater), the moralist, or the religious Jew, the verdict is the same: Man stands condemned before God and in need of a redemption which he is unable to gain by his own efforts (3:19, 20).

"But now," says Paul (3:21, 22) in a note of exaltation, "has God provided a righteousness apart from law" (i.e., man's best efforts). This is the truth of justification by faith in the redeeming work of Christ. The one who places his faith in Him is justified, and the apostle shows the supreme example in Abraham who "believed God and it was counted to him for righteousness." To "justify" means to "declare righteous" before God. This is made possible because God imputes, or reckons, to the believer the righteousness of His Son as by faith the individual indentifies himself with his Substitute (cf. also I Cor. 1:30). Certain results accrue from this act of justification (5:1-11) and the basis is found in the contrast between Christ and Adam in 5:12-21.

After spelling out what God has done and magnifying the grace of God in salvation, Paul begins to apply the effect of the Cross to the life of the believer. The truth of justification, which is a legal act, is carried forward to sanctification, which is concerned primarily with the believer's life or experience. While "Christ has been made unto us sanctification," we are correspondingly to appropriate this provision. Chapter 6 describes the basis of sanctification: Our union with Christ in His death and resurrection. This is to be taken by faith (6:11) and, in the light of such a truth, the believer is to yield himself to God as a servant of righteousness (6:12 ff.). Such will not be accomplished easily. The great struggle between the old and new natures in the believer is described in chapter 7, and victory through the operation of "the law of the Spirit of life" in chapter 8.

Paul declares that freedom from the condemnation of the law is realized to the one who is "in Christ" (8:1) and who walks "not after the flesh but after the Spirit" (8:4). The Holy Spirit is also the mark of divine sonship (8:9), the One who bears witness of relationship to God (8:16) and the Intercessor in prayer (8:26, 27). A final note of assurance is given in 8:35-39 in that "nothing can separate us from the love of Christ."

The fourth aspect of redemption is its *scope:* It reaches out to include both Jew and Gentile. The Gospel is a *universal* message. As the promise was given through Abraham and his seed, Paul takes this people of Israel as his starting point. He clearly portrays their past, with its glories and failures; their present, with God's call of salvation; and their future, with the promise that "all Israel shall be saved." But this is not a sectarian spirit. "Whosoever shall call on the name of the Lord shall be saved" (10:13), and the Gentiles are objects of God's mercy as well.

Finally, the believer, as a justified, sanctified, dedicated individual, is to serve God. The mercies of God are the expression of the heart of God and are designed to bring about a dedication of the believer's body and mind (12:1, 2). Building on all that has been said in chapters 1-11, Paul lays before the believer his responsibilities in the area of the church (12:3-8), individual relationships (12:9-21), the state (13:1-7), society (13:8-12), and personal convictions (14:1—15:13).

The concluding part of the letter (15:14—16:27) is mainly an expression of Paul's hopes to visit Rome, his plans for further evangelistic efforts and greetings to personal friends in the church.

Thus the apostle has defined at length the Gospel of the grace of God. It is a far-reaching message. It probes deeply into the heart of man, provides a positive answer to the problem of sin and challenges the believer to live a life of dedication and service.

Suggested Readings

CORINTHIANS

Grosheide, F. W. *Commentary on the First Epistle to the Corinthians* in *The New International Commentary on the New Testament.* Grand Rapids: Wm. B. Eerdmans Publishing Co., 1953.

Morgan, G. C. *The Corinthian Letters of Paul.* New York: Fleming H. Revell Company.

Robertson, A. and Plummer, A. *The First Epistle of St. Paul to the Corinthians* in *The International Critical Commentary.* Edinburgh: T. & T. Clark, 1953. Thorough commentary on the Greek text.

GALATIANS

Hogg, C. F. and Vine, W. E. *The Epistle to the Galatians with Notes Exegetical and Expository.* London: Pickering & Inglis, Ltd., 1959.

Lightfoot, J. B. *Saint Paul's Epistle to the Galatians.* London: Macmillan and Co., Ltd., 1896. Advanced commentary on the Greek text. Special notes and dissertations added.

Tenney, M. C. *Galatians: The Charter of Christian Liberty.* Revised and Enlarged Edition. Grand Rapids: Wm. B. Eerdmans Publishing Co., 1957. Chapters illustrating ten methods of Bible study applied to Galatians.

ROMANS

Godet, F. *Commentary on the Epistle to the Romans.* Grand Rapids: Zondervan Publishing House, 1956 (reprint).

Moule, H. C. G. *The Epistle to the Romans.* London: Pickering & Inglis, Ltd., n.d. Excellent theological discussions following verse-by-verse comments.

Murray, J. *Commentary on the Epistle to the Romans* in *The New International Commentary on the New Testament.* Chapters 1-8. Grand Rapids: Wm. B. Eerdmans Publishing Co., 1960. Highly recommended.

Newell, W. R. *Romans Verse by Verse.* Chicago: Moody Press, n.d.

Thomas, W. H. G. *St. Paul's Epistle to the Romans.* Grand Rapids: Wm. B. Eerdmans Publishing Co., 1953 (reprint).

CHAPTER 11

THE PAULINE EPISTLES:
CHRISTOLOGICAL

Introduction

A CCORDING to the last verses of Acts, Paul spent two years "in his own hired house," a prisoner of the Roman government. As a Roman citizen, he had appealed to Caesar (Acts 25:11), and was awaiting opportunity of pleading his case before the emperor. During these days the apostle was allowed to carry on his ministry of teaching and preaching within the confines of his prison,[1] and he bears testimony to the fact that God had honored his labors. In Philippians 1:13 and 4:22 are found saints "of Caesar's household."

His ministry was not only oral, however. From this period come some of the richest and most profound of his writings, the so-called Prison Epistles. Colossians and Ephesians are the "twin Epistles" of the Pauline collection; Philemon is a personal letter, sent to a slave-owner in Colossae; Philippians, although addressed to a church, is personal in tone and full of expressions of Christian joy. All of them emphasize the Person of Christ and contain, directly or by implication, profound theological expressions of the nature and mission of the Son of God (see esp. Col. 1:15-22; Eph. 1:20-23; Phil. 2:5-11).

Tradition states that these Epistles were written while Paul was a prisoner in Rome. That he was a prisoner may certainly be affirmed on the basis of the Epistles themselves (Col. 1:24; Eph. 3:1; 4:1; 6:20; Philem. 1, 9, 10; Phil. 1:12, 13). In addition, the references to the "praetorian guard" and "Caesar's

---

[1]D. A. Hayes, *Paul and His Epistles* (New York: Methodist Book Concern, 1919), p. 333, suggests, with a touch of wit, that Paul held cottage meetings in his humble home "and made it the Saint Paul's Cathedral of his day" (!).

household" in Philippians fit better with Rome than else-where.[2]

The chronological order of the Epistles is disputed. Philip-pians has been placed both first and last; Colossians has been put both before and after Ephesians. Consequently, the ar-rangement here is somewhat arbitrary. The letter to Colossians will be treated first, followed by Ephesians and Philemon, then Philippians, a fitting climax to the writings from prison.

COLOSSIANS

Among the Epistles of Paul, only Colossians and Romans were written to churches which had not been founded or estab-lished by the apostle (Rom. 1:10-13; 15:23, 24; Col. 2:1). It seems likely that the Colossian Church, which met in the home of Philemon (Philem. 1), was the fruit of Paul's Ephesian stay (Acts 19:10), and that Epaphras was the one primarily re-sponsible for beginning the work (Col. 1:7, 8; 4:12, 13).

Date and Destination

On his third missionary venture, Paul spent a long period at Ephesus, self-confessed "mother of Asia." From this crucial center, the province at large was reached with the Gospel. Following Paul's arrest in Jerusalem, upon his return from the third journey (Acts 21:30-36), he was taken to Caesarea and then to Rome. While Paul was in Rome (Acts 28:30, 31), Epaphras came to him from Colossae to report the conditions in the Church (Col. 1:8; 2:4, ff.). If the imprisonment at Rome is correctly dated at about A.D. 60-62, this letter may be placed about 60/61. It was probably taken to Colossae, along with the letter to Philemon, by Tychicus and Onesimus (Col. 4:7-9).

In the first century A.D., Colossae was a small city in Phrygia, in Asia Minor. It was located on the southern bank of the river Lycus, and was neighbor to the more prominent cities of Laodicea and Hierapolis (Col. 2:1; 4:13, 16).[3] Lying on the

---

[2]M. C. Tenney, *The New Testament* (Grand Rapids: Wm. B. Eerdmans Pub. Co., 1953), p. 329. See also David Smith, *Life and Letters of St. Paul* (London: Hodder & Stoughton, 1919), pp. 504-507.

[3]D. A. Hayes, *op. cit.*, pp. 351-354, gives an interesting descriptive sum-mary of the three cities. Laodicea was "the metropolis of the valley," Hier-apolis was "the sacred city," but Colossae "surely is the least important place to which any of Paul's letters were written" (p. 354).

main trade route between Ephesus and the East, it was subject
to the influence of both western and eastern ideologies.

Purpose

As was usually the case, Paul wrote to express his earnest
desire for the spiritual welfare of these people and to assure
them of his constant prayers (1:9, ff.). But there had arisen a
serious threat to the doctrinal foundation of the Church, the
so-called "Colossian heresy," and the apostle hastens to point
out the danger and the solution to it.[4] This treatment (2:8-
3:4) makes up the heart of the Epistle. Along with this section should be read carefully 1:15-22, which is Paul's exposition of the person and work of Christ.

Outline

The answer to the problems faced in this letter is a superior
Christology. A key verse is 1:18 in which Paul stated, "That
in all things he might have the pre-eminence." The underlying
theme of the Epistle is the supremacy of Christ as Head of the
Church.

I. Salutation	1:1, 2
II. The Prayer of Thanksgiving	1:3-8
III. The Prayer of Intercession	1:9-14
IV. The Supremacy of Christ	1:15-23
V. Paul's Desire for the Saints	1:24—2:7
VI. Paul's Exhortations to the Saints	2:8—4:6
1. To guard against false philosophy	2:8-15
2. To guard against false worship	2:16-19
3. To guard against false asceticism	2:20—3:4

---

[4]One of the classic treatments of the subject is that found in Bishop
Lightfoot's commentary, *St. Paul's Epistles to the Colossians and Philemon*
(London: Macmillan and Co., Ltd., 1886), pp. 71-111. See also E. K. Simp-
son and F. F. Bruce, *Commentary on the Epistles to the Ephesians and the
Colossians* in *The New International Commentary* series (Grand Rapids:
Eerdmans, 1958), pp. 165-173. The specific characteristics of the heresy
are dealt with in the summary of the epistle which follows.

4. To attain Christian maturity   3:5-17
5. To follow right conduct   3:18—4:1
6. To practice continual prayer   4:2-6

VII. Paul's Representatives to Colossae   4:7-9

VIII. Greetings   4:10-17

IX. Conclusion   4:18

Paul does not argue in this Epistle. His approach to the Colossians is to show in a positive way the superiority of Christ. In the first chapter, Christ is presented as pre-eminent in relation to His Father (v. 15), the creation (vv. 15-17), the Church (v. 18) and redemption (vv. 19-23).[5]

In 2:8—3:4, the "Colossian heresy" is exposed. Because it is not systematically treated by Paul, the complete picture is not easily ascertained, but the following characteristics are observable: 1) *a false philosophy* which was based on rationalism rather than revelation (v. 8). The answer to this is given in verses 9 on: in Christ the fullness of the Godhead resides and is revealed. 2) *A legalistic religion* was threatening to engulf the realities of Christian freedom (v. 16). Paul's reply is that these things are only shadows while the substance, the fulfillment, is found in Christ (v. 17). 3) *A mystical asceticism and angel-worship* which introduced a false object of worship (cf. v. 19, "not holding fast the Head") was condemned by Paul as "fleshly" (v. 23) and of no value in true spiritual relationships. Christ is "our life" (3:4) and "the things that are above" (3:1) are to occupy the Christian consciousness.

What was the source of this heresy? Bruce has summed it up stating, "We must probably think of this cult as an ingredient of non-Jewish provenience in the amalgam of Jewish legalism

---

[5] In this passage the following terms should be carefully observed: "image" (v. 15), a copy or reflection of an archetype (cf. II Cor. 4:4); "firstborn of all creation" (v. 15), the one who exercises the privilege of primogeniture (cf. Heb. 1:2); "the beginning" (v. 18), a reference to pre-existence, involving the ideas of priority in time and the power of originating (cf. I Cor. 15:20, 23; Acts 3:14); "the first born from the dead" (v. 18), the Lord of life and death (cf. Rev. 1:5; Rom. 8:29; Heb. 2:14f.). For details see Simpson and Bruce, *ibid.*, pp. 192-206; Lightfoot, *op. cit.*, pp. 142-156, and the lexicons.

and Gnostic asceticism which we call the Colossian heresy."[6]

The remainder of the Epistle is primarily concerned with the character and conduct of the believer. The "old man" with his deeds (3:5-9) is to be "put off"; the "new man" is to govern the Christian in his conduct (3:10-17). Applying these principles to the domestic scene, Paul addresses three pairs of individuals, giving appropriate instruction to each:

1. Wives, be in subjection to your husbands   3:18
   Husbands, love your wives   3:19
2. Children, obey your parents in all things   3:20
   Fathers, do not provoke your children   3:21
3. Servants, obey your masters in all things   3:22-25
   Masters, treat your servants justly   4:1

A word may be added concerning some of the persons named in 4:7-17. Both Tychicus and Onesimus, the bearers of the Epistle, are highly commended by Paul. Tychicus is 1) the beloved brother, 2) faithful minister and 3) fellow-servant in the Lord. Onesimus is 1) the faithful and 2) beloved brother and 3) one of you, of the Colossian Church. Mark (John Mark of Acts 12:12; 13:5) is rightly described by the American Standard Version as "the cousin of Barnabas" (not "sister's son" as in A.V.). Archippus may be the same man mentioned in Philemon 1. Apparently he had been dilatory in carrying out his responsibilities. Paul crisply exhorts him, "Take heed to the ministry which thou hast received in the Lord, that thou fulfill it" (4:17).

EPHESIANS

In Ephesians, Paul "surveys the purposes of God from eternity to eternity. This Epistle bids us look behind and beyond,

---

[6]*Op. cit.*, p. 248. For a full discussion see the same work, pp. 243-263. Some verbal parallels between Paul's terminology used to describe this heresy and the language of the Qumran scrolls has been noted by W. D. Davies, "Paul and the Dead Sea Scrolls," in *The Scrolls and the New Testament*, edited by K. Stendahl (N. Y.: Harper & Brothers, 1957), pp. 165-169. He adds a word of caution as to identifying the sources of the heresy too closely, but adds, "Nevertheless, along with the other factors mentioned above, it would seem that the forces of evil in Colossians may be the same as those referred to in the Scrolls" (p. 168).

into the infinite."[7] As the reader scans the writings of the apostle, he is caught by the feeling that this letter is the most profound of them all. Its key phrase is "in heavenly places" (lit., "in the heavenlies," 1:3, 10, 20; 2:6; 3:10; 6:12). Its view of the Church is not the church local but the Church universal. Every true believer united by faith with Christ forms a part of that Church, "which is his body" and of which He is the Head (1:22, 23).

Date and Destination

As has been noted previously, Ephesians is one of the prison epistles and may therefore be dated about A.D. 60/61. In this case the destination is a more vexing issue. To whom was the letter originally addressed?

While the phrase "at Ephesus" appears in many of our printed versions, the words are curiously omitted in the two oldest manuscripts of the New Testament, the Vaticanus (B) and the Sinaiticus (ℵ).[8] It is not impossible that the original address may have been "to the saints which are, and to the faithful in Christ Jesus" (1:1). Aside from the likely possibility that the original address "at Ephesus" may have been dropped out of some manuscripts, three other major suggestions have been made to answer the problem.

1. The Epistle was intended to be a "circular letter" to the churches in the province of Asia, and a blank space was left after the words, "to the saints which are," in verse 1. In this way the name of any particular church could be supplied. Ephesus, being the "mother church" of Asia, had her name preserved in most manuscripts.

2. Some have suggested that this was "the Epistle from Laodicea" referred to in Colossians 4:16. As Colossians and "Ephesians" are the "twin Epistles," due to their many similarities, it would seem possible thus to identify "Ephesians." The alternatives, of course, are to say that the Laodicean Epistle has been

---

[7]Scroggie, op. cit., p. 210.
[8]Both manuscripts are dated in the first half of the fourth century, and are the two most important manuscripts discovered to date. The former is in the Vatican library in Rome, the latter in the British Museum in London.

lost or that it was only one copy of the circular letter as described above.

3. Still others have asserted that "Ephesians" was intended to be a "universal Epistle" addressed to "the saints" and "the faithful" in any Church. While the lack of local references would seem to give a measure of credence to this view, yet the remarks of Paul in such passages as 1:15 ff. and 6:22 seem to indicate a definite group in Paul's mind.

Even though the circular theory has become a popular one, the traditional view—that it was directed specifically to Ephesus—has much to be said for it and is assumed in the remarks that follow.[9]

The city of Ephesus was, in the first century A.D., the leading city of the Roman province of Asia. While Pergamum retained its place as the official capital of the province,[10] her neighbor to the south was fast replacing her in most other respects. Ephesus was prominent in several respects.

1. *Religiously,* she was the proud possessor of the temple of Diana (the Greek Artemis), which was one of the seven wonders of the ancient world. More than 340 feet long and 160 feet wide and containing 100 columns each over 55 feet high,[11] the marble temple glistened in the sunlight and attracted worshipers from near and far. An image of the goddess was within the inner shrine, a gold-covered figure covered with many breasts, because she was the symbol of fertility. Acts 19:35 relates that the Ephesians spoke of the statue as having "fallen from Jupiter." It may have been carved from a meteorite which had at some ancient time fallen from the

---

[9]For good discussion of the Ephesian letter, see D. E. Hiebert, *An Introduction to the Pauline Epistles* (Chicago: Moody Press, 1954), pp. 254-282; D. A. Hayes, *op. cit.*, pp. 381-403. Hiebert maintains the Ephesian destination, Hayes the circular idea. Both books contain good analyses of the characteristics of the Epistle.

[10]Although Ephesus is called the capital of Asia by a number of writers (J. A. Robinson, E. K. Simpson, *et al.*), Ramsay has emphasized that Pergamum still retained this place. See Ramsay, *The Letters to the Seven Churches of Asia* (London: Hodder & Stoughton, n.d.), p. 227: "In the Roman province of Asia, Pergamum, the old capital of the Kings, continued to be the titular capital . . ."; p. 283: ". . . its history as the seat of supreme authority over a large country lasts about four centuries, and had not yet come to an end when the Seven Letters were written."

[11]G. E. Wright, *Biblical Archeology* (Philadelphia: The Westminster Press, 1957), p. 253.

sky. Demetrius and his silversmiths carried on a brisk trade manufacturing and selling the small silver shrines to the tourists (Acts 19:24, 25). Closely related to the worship of Artemis in Ephesus was the active "cult of Augustus" in honor of the Emperor.[12] A third feature was the practice of magic, closely related to the worship of Diana, and described briefly in Acts 19:19. The story of the sons of Sceva (Acts 19:13-16) shows that added to all this was traffic in evil spirits (cf. Eph. 6:12).

2. *Commercially,* Ephesus was ranked with Alexandria (Egypt) and Antioch (Syria) as one of the three leading centers of trade in the Eastern Mediterranean.[13] Located near the mouth of the river Cayster, her position was strategic. A channel connected her with the sea, and ships from every nation were found in her port.

3. *Intellectually,* she boasted of leaders in philosophy, poetry, painting, oratory and other fields.[14] Her prominence in architecture has already been noted in the Ephesian temple.

Purpose

No specific indication of purpose is contained within the Epistle itself. It is not polemic as is its twin, Colossians. Paul appears to be expounding the doctrine of the Church universal as a basis for a proper understanding of its nature and purpose in the world. In this way the local Churches would be able to view themselves as parts of "the Church, which is his body."

Outline

The "Epistle of the Church" may be analyzed as follows:

I. Salutation	1:1, 2
II. The Church in the Purpose of God	1:3-14
1. Work of the Father	1:3-6

---

[12]A shrine and a great altar of Augustus was placed in the Ephesian temple soon after his accession. This was a local cult, and was followed by Provincial temples of other Roman emperors. See Ramsay, *op. cit.,* pp. 231, 232.

[13]Hiebert, *op. cit.,* p. 254.

[14]David Smith, *The Life and Letters of St. Paul* (London: Hodder & Stoughton, 1919), p. 226.

2. Work of the Son   1:6-12
3. Work of the Spirit   1:13,14

III. The Church and the Power of God   1:15—2:10
1. Illustrated in the quickening of Christ   1:15-23
2. Realized in the quickening of sinners   2:1-10

IV. The Church as the Household of God   2:11-22

V. The Church as the Revelation of God   3:1-13
1. The mystery of Christ   3:1-9
2. The wisdom of God   3:10-13

VI. The Church and the Fullness of God   3:14-21

VII. The Church and the Standards of God ·   4:1—6:9
1. The plea for spiritual unity   4:1-16
2. The demand for moral purity   4:17—5:21
3. The obligations of domestic duty   5:22—6:9

VIII. The Church and the Armor of God   6:10-20
1. The exhortation   6:10, 11
2. The enemy   6:12, 13
3. The equipment   6:14-20

IX. Conclusion   6:21-24

One of the most profound passages to be found in Scripture is that in 1:3-14. Paul reaches back into eternity to describe what God has done; expounds the doctrines of election, predestination, redemption, adoption and the work of the Holy Spirit; and concludes by stating that God will both "sum up all things in Christ" and will finally redeem "the purchased possession." The recurring phrase "to the praise of His glory" (1:6, 12, 14) provides a framework for the description of the Divine activity, centering in the work of the Father, Son and Holy Spirit, respectively.[15]

Paul follows by uttering one of his majestic prayers (1:15 ff.), that the believers may have spiritual insight to realize 1)

---

[15]The sealing of the believer (1:13) by the Holy Spirit, who is Himself the seal, is God's pledge of final redemption. The term "earnest" is a colorful one, not only used in business transactions as a "pledge" but in personal relations as "an engagement ring." The term still persists in modern Greek. (Other N. T. occurrences II Cor. 1:22; 5:5.)

the hope of His calling, 2) the divine inheritance in the saints and 3) the greatness of God's power.[16] This power has been exercised in raising Christ from the dead and exalting Him to Headship of the Church (1:20-23), and the same power has been manifested in regenerating the one "dead in sin" (2:1 ff.). The practical evidence of this new life, according to God's purpose, is a life of good works (2:10).

The Church is composed of both Jew and Gentile, made one through the breaking down of "the middle wall of partition" (2:14). This is the result of the redemptive work of Christ who "is our peace" (2:14), "has made peace" (2:15), and "came and preached peace" (2:17). Consequently, this new body is described as "the household of God" (2:19), "a holy temple in the Lord" (2:21), and "a habitation of God in the Spirit" (2:22).

By way of explaining what all this means, Paul goes on to say that the truth concerning the Church was not made known to "other generations" but has "now been revealed unto His holy apostles and prophets" (3:5). The mystery being made plain, it is now known that the Gentiles are "fellow-heirs, and fellow-members of the body, and fellow-partakers of the promise in Christ Jesus through the gospel" (3:6). Following this exposition, the apostle falls to his knees (3:14) and prays that God will grant the realization of His power and love to every believer.

The remainder of the Epistle is concerned with the believer's daily experience in the light of the divine provisions. One of the keys used in opening this door into the Christian life is the word "walk," which occurs in a total of seven passages in the Epistle:

The walk in sin	2:2
The walk in good works	2:10
The walk in unity	4:1-3

[16]The greatest concentration of words for "power" anywhere to be found in the New Testament occurs in 1:19. Four of the five usual terms are employed in this single verse: 1) "power" (*dynamis*) has reference to inherent or *potential* power; 2) "working" (*energeia*) to *active* power; 3) "strength" (*kratos*) to power as *mastery* and 4) "might" (*ischyos*) to power *in manifestation.*

The walk in newness of life	4:17 ff.
The walk in love	5:2
The walk in light	5:8
The walk in wisdom	5:15

The standards of God for the believer first demand *unity* (4:3); to assure the realization of this unity spiritual gifts have been provided (4:11). Those persons in the Church who possess such gifts are to bring the believers generally to a state of maturity, then each believer in turn is to carry on the work of ministering and edification (4:12).

Further, the standards of God demand *purity*. The "old man" is to be put away; the "new man" is to be put on (4:22-24). This finds expression in the many avenues of human relationships. It is "giving feet" to one's beliefs! Such conduct marks the Spirit-filled life—the kind of conduct epitomized in joy, thanksgiving and subjection to one another (5:18-21).

Coming to the domestic scene, Paul sets forth the demands of *duty* upon those within the home (5:22—6:9).[17] Here in Ephesians the distinctive feature is that the union of husband and wife is used to illustrate the relationship of Christ and the Church (5:32).

The closing exhortation of the Epistle deals with the believer as a soldier. He is admonished to be strong in the Lord. He is warned that his enemy is not physical but spiritual. He is instructed in the use of the "whole armor of God." The significance of the armor may be briefly summarized as follows:

The leather belt—	
rightness of heart	(cf. Isa. 11:5; Ps. 51:6)
The breastplate—rightness expressed	(cf. Isa. 59:17)
The shoes—	
a ready message	(cf. Rom. 10:15; I Peter 3:15)
The shield—a vital trust in God	(cf. Ps. 18:2)
The helmet—	
protection of the mind	(cf. Isa. 59:17; I Thess. 5:8)
The sword—the Word of God	(cf. Heb. 4:12)

---

[17]Cf. Col. 3:18—4:1.

All this is available to the believer, but it must be "taken up" and "put on."

So Paul has led his readers from the initial design in God's mind to the daily life of the redeemed individual. With a firm grasp upon the great truth of the Church, the believer is to walk worthy of his calling.

PHILEMON

Preserved in the Epistle to Philemon is a sample of Paul's personal correspondence.[18] It is a classic letter and contains a striking example of Christian brotherhood and the meaning of forgiveness.

Date and Destination

The letter, along with Colossians, may be dated at A.D. 60/61. It was carried to its destination by Tychicus and Onesimus.

Purpose

While a prisoner in Rome, Paul came in contact with a runaway slave, Onesimus, and led him to Christ (Philem. 10). From the contents of the letter, it would seem that the man had robbed his master (18), and then fled to Rome. Although Paul would have been pleased to keep Onesimus with him in Rome (13), he felt that the slave should be returned to his master. To offset the possible punishment that Onesimus might receive,[19] this letter was written, tenderly requesting that he would be received "not now as a servant, but more than a servant, a brother beloved . . ." (16).

---

[18]"Probably he wrote scores of these private letters, but all of the others have perished. This single surviving specimen shows that Paul was both a gentleman and a saint, and we may judge from it that if we had a complete collection of the lesser and private Pauline epistles, we would find that they would rank with those of Luther and of Rutherford as a distinct addition to the engaging devotional literature of the church." D. A. Hayes, *Paul and His Epistles* (New York: Methodist Book Concern, 1919), p. 335.

[19]A slave (*doulos*) was regarded as the absolute property of his master, and was subject completely to him. It was not unthinkable, therefore, that a slave who robbed his owner would be put to death by crucifixion when apprehended, or at least punished very severely. This was Onesimus' due, but Paul interceded for him.

Outline

The theme of the letter is the idea of forgiveness on the basis of brotherhood in Christ (8, 16).

I. Salutation   1-3

II. The Prayer for Philemon's Ministry   4-7

III. The Petition for Onesimus' Restoration   8-21

IV. The Prospect of Paul's Visit   22

V. Conclusion   23-25

The name, Onesimus, in itself is an interesting word, meaning "profitable." As Paul recalled the past history of this man, he said he was "once to thee unprofitable, but now profitable to thee and to me" (11). No longer, then, was he simply a servant, but now, in addition, a "brother beloved."

But what of Onesimus' debt to his master? The answer to this problem is the crux of the letter. In verses 18 and 19 Paul says, "Put that [the debt] on mine account; I Paul have written *it* with mine own hand, I will repay *it*."[20] Both these expressions were current in the papyri of the first century, and were used in bookkeeping procedures and legal involvements.[21] Paul puts himself in the place of Onesimus and asks Philemon, "receive him as myself" (17). From a theological standpoint, this expression illustrates the doctrine of *imputation*. The debt of Onesimus is placed to Paul's account; the character of Paul is placed to Onesimus' account, and he is thereby accepted by his master. As has been noted by Tenney,[22] all the elements of divine forgiveness are herein illustrated: the offense (11, 18),

---

[20]Lightfoot, *op. cit.*, p. 341, translates verses 18 and 19 as follows: "But if he has done thee any injury, or if he stands in thy debt, set it down to my account. Here is my signature—*Paul*—in my own handwriting. Accept this as my bond. I will repay thee."

[21]See Moulton and Milligan, *The Vocabulary of the Greek Testament*, London: Hodder & Stoughton, Ltd., 1952, p. 204, where the "putting to one's account" is illustrated from the papyri, and p. 71, where the expression, "I will repay," is said to carry "the idea of repayment by way of punishment or fine."

[22]*Op. cit.*, p. 331.

compassion (10), intercession (10, 18, 19), substitution (18, 19), restoration to favor (15), and elevation to a new relationship."

PHILIPPIANS

This is the most pleasantly personal church Epistle which has come from Paul's pen. He writes with a sense of gratitude and devotion to friends close to his heart. This is all the more remarkable in view of the circumstances which surrounded the letter.

From the account in Acts 16, it will be recalled that Philippi was the first preaching point in Paul's European itinerary. In response to the vision at Troas, in which the man of Macedonia pleaded, "Come over into Macedonia, and help us" (Acts 16: 9), Paul crossed the sea and began his ministry in Philippi. After a successful beginning, which saw the conversion of Lydia and others, Paul and Silas, his companion, were falsely accused of being subversionists, severely beaten and imprisoned. Although freed the next day, their wounds bore grim witness to the beginnings of their labors in this city.

Now, ten or more years afterward, Paul was in Rome—again a prisoner! While his physical circumstances were more favorable than in the Philippian prison, nonetheless he was in a state of confinement. In the face of these two imprisonments and their accompanying discomforts, it is, as has been said, the more remarkable that the key words of the Epistle are *joy* and *rejoice*! Paul further adds, "I have learned, in whatsoever state I am, *therewith* to be content" (4:11). This is a radiant testimony to the reality of Christian faith.

Date and Destination

The dating of Philippians and its relation to the other Prison Epistles is somewhat conjectural, but placing it last and dating it about A.D. 61 will not be far afield.[23]

The address of the letter is unique. It was sent "to all the

---

[23]Hayes, *op. cit.*, pp. 430-433, argues convincingly for this order, following the other three Epistles. He assigns a slightly later date, however, A.D. 63 or 64.

saints in Christ Jesus which are at Philippi, with the bishops and deacons" (1:1). Only here is such an address to be found. It reflects the basic organizational features of the early Churches, and forms a fitting introduction to the last group of Paul's Epistles (esp. I Tim. and Titus) which contain detailed instructions for the appointment of these Church officers.

Philippi itself was an interesting city. In Luke's record of Paul's journeys, it is the only city which is described for the reader. Acts 16:12 relates that Philippi was 1) "a city of Macedonia," 2) "the first of the district" and 3) "a *Roman* colony." The province called Macedonia had long been famed as the home of King Philip and his more famous son, Alexander the Great. After subduing the province in 168 B.C., the Romans divided it into four districts, Philippi lying within the First District on the borders of Thrace. When, in 42 B.C., during the Roman civil wars, Antony and Octavian (later Augustus) defeated Brutus and Cassius on this site, Philippi was awarded the status of a Roman colony.[24] The pride of the people of this city in "being Romans" is clearly seen in Acts 16:20, 21. There was no synagogue in Philippi which probably meant that there were few Jews resident there, as only ten Jewish men were needed to constitute a synagogue.[25]

Purpose

Paul wrote to thank the Philippian Church for the gift they had sent to him by Epaphroditus (2:25; 4:10, 14). Their generosity and concern over the welfare of the apostle had been manifested on at least three other occasions. Twice they had sent a gift to him at Thessalonica (4:15, 16) and once to Corinth (II Cor. 11:9).

There is also included the plea for oneness of mind through true humility. This spirit is illustrated in the humiliation of Christ, followed by His exaltation (2:1-11). A specific ex-

---

[24]For further detail, see F. F. Bruce, *Commentary on the Book of Acts* in the *New International Commentary on the New Testament* (Grand Rapids: Wm. B. Eerdmans, 1954), p. 330 and footnotes.

[25]Bruce, *ibid.*, p. 331 and footnote. The Jews who appear in Acts 16 are women, and as Bruce notes, they were of no account in the number needed for the establishment of a house of worship!

ample of an existing lack of unity is given in 4:2, where two of the prominent women of the Church are exhorted to be "of the same mind" (cf. 2:2, 3).

Outline

The Gospel of Christ is intended to shape both the attitudes and the actions of believers. True joy is linked with humility of spirit and oneness of mind. These characteristics are illustrated in the lives of the leading personalities of the Epistle. The twofold theme of "good news" (Gospel) and "joy" characterize the entire Epistle.

I.	Salutation	1:1, 2
II.	Thanksgiving and Prayer for the Saints	1:3-11
III.	Paul and His Circumstances	1:12-26
IV.	Believers and Their Conduct	1:27-30
V.	Christ and His Example: Humility	2:1-18
VI.	Timothy and Epaphroditus and Their Concern	2:19-30
VII.	Paul and His Example: Maturity	3:1—4:1
VIII.	Exhortations and Appreciation	4:2-20
IX.	Conclusion	4:21-23

As Paul writes this Epistle, he is able to rejoice, even though he is imprisoned. The reason is not far to seek. Christ is being preached (1:18)![26] Although some preach out of "envy and strife," yet others, emboldened by Paul's example, preach out of love. At any rate, the preaching continues. But it is important, not only that the Gospel should be preached, but also that it should be lived. Hence follows the exhortation to live in such a manner as to be "worthy of the gospel of Christ" (1:27).[27]

The plea for unity through genuine humility occupies much

---

[26]Paul's anticipation of release (1:19) and the gift from Philippi (4:10-18) were also reasons for rejoicing.

[27]See the similar exhortations in Ephesians 4:1 and II Peter 3:11. Jesus' exhortation to His disciples in Matthew 5:16 is in the same vein.

of the second chapter (2:1-18). Following a description of the *meaning* of humility (2:1-4), Paul gives an illustration of the idea (2:5-11). Christ has exemplified this attitude in His self-humbling, even to the extent of death. He who had the prerogatives of Deity voluntarily laid them aside to assume the role of a servant and do the will of His Father here on the earth.[28] Then the *application* is made: ". . . work out your own salvation with fear and trembling; for it is God who worketh in you . . . to will and to work for his good pleasure" (2:12, 13, A.S.V.).

The next major hortatory section is Paul's plea for maturity (3:1—4:1). Based on his own example, which illustrates the failure of legalistic righteousness and the discovery of true life in Christ, Paul exhorts the Philippians to "be thus minded." In 3:8, "that I may gain Christ"; in 3:9, to "be found in him," and in 3:10, "that I may know Him," sums up Paul's life goal. "Philippians depicts a totalitarian life in Christ."[29]

Four practical exhortations close the Epistle. Likemindedness in the work of the Lord (4:2, 3), the absence of anxiety through trust in God (4:6, 7), pure thoughts (4:8), and contentment in the material realm (4:10-19) are all qualities which should characterize the believer.

Suggested Readings

COLOSSIANS AND PHILEMON

Lightfoot, J. B. *Saint Paul's Epistles to the Colossians and to Philemon.* London: Macmillan and Co., Ltd., 1886. Greek text. Extensive introduction and special notes and dissertations.

---

[28]Countless pages have been written in an attempt to define the meaning of the phrase, "emptied himself" (2:7). It is quite in keeping with the context and the rest of Scripture to say that Christ voluntarily assumed a state of self-limitation for the purposes of redemption. Consequently, He was exalted by the Father and, says Paul, all "shall confess that Jesus Christ is Lord" (2:11). For a thorough discussion of the passage see J. B. Lightfoot, *The Epistle of St. Paul to the Philippians* (London: Macmillan & Co., Ltd., 1903), pp. 110-115, and special note, pp. 127-137, dealing with the terms "form" and "fashion." A. B. Bruce, *The Humiliation of Christ* (Grand Rapids: Wm. B. Eerdmans, 1955), deals at length with the many theories and problems of the subject.

[29]M. C. Tenney, *The New Testament: An Historical and Analytical Survey* (Grand Rapids: Eerdmans, 1953), p. 339.

Moule, H. C. G. *Colossian and Philemon Studies.* London: Pickering & Inglis, n.d.

Williams, A. L. *The Epistles of Paul the Apostle to the Colossians and to Philemon* in the *Cambridge Greek Testament.* Cambridge: Cambridge University Press, 1928.

EPHESIANS

Moule, H. C. G. *Ephesian Studies.* London: Hodder and Stoughton, 1900.

Robinson, J. A. *St. Paul's Epistle to the Ephesians.* Second Edition. London: Macmillan and Company, Ltd., 1907. Exposition of the English text followed by analysis of the Greek text.

Simpson, E. K. and Bruce, F. F. *Commentary on the Epistles to the Ephesians and the Colossians* in *The New International Commentary on the New Testament.* Grand Rapids: Wm. B. Eerdmans Publishing Co., 1957.

Westcott, B. F. *Saint Paul's Epistle to the Ephesians: The Greek Text with Notes and Addenda.* London: Macmillan and Company, Ltd., 1906.

PHILIPPIANS

Lightfoot, J. B. *Saint Paul's Epistle to the Philippians.* London: Macmillan and Company, Ltd., 1903. Greek text and special dissertations.

Moule, H. C. G., ed. *The Epistle of Paul the Apostle to the Philippians* in *The Cambridge Greek Testament for Schools and Colleges.* Cambridge: Cambridge University Press, 1923. Helpful word studies.

Moule, H. C. G. *Philippian Studies.* London: Pickering & Inglis, Ltd., n.d.

Rees, P. S. *The Adequate Man: Paul in Philippians.* Westwood, N. J.: Fleming H. Revell Co., 1959. Readable and practical exposition.

Tenney, M. C. *Philippians: The Gospel at Work.* Grand Rapids: Wm. B. Eerdmans Publishing Co., 1956.

Vincent, M. R. *A Critical and Exegetical Commentary on the Epistles to the Philippians and to Philemon* in the *International Critical Commentary.* New York: Charles Scribner's Sons, 1906.

CHAPTER 12

THE PAULINE EPISTLES: ECCLESIOLOGICAL

Introduction

THE FOURTH GROUP of the Pauline Epistles, commonly called the "Pastoral Epistles," deals primarily with matters related to the governing and functioning of local churches and the responsibilities of their duly appointed leaders. They were addressed to two of Paul's companions and fellow-workers: Timothy, who resided at Ephesus (I Tim. 1:3), and Titus, who had been left by Paul in Crete (Titus 1:5).

Problem of Authorship

This critical question, common to the three Epistles, should be discussed briefly at this point. Although the testimony of the Church, with respect to Pauline authorship, was unanimous from the second century onward, critics began to question their authenticity early in the nineteenth century.[1]

On the basis of internal evidence, several types of objections have been raised by scholars. They may be broken down into four major categories: historical, linguistic, doctrinal and ecclesiastical.[2]

---

[1]Marcion, a heretic of the second century, seems to be the chief critic of these three Epistles in the early Church. As the Epistles condemned many of the practices of Marcion, it is not difficult to understand his attitude. "A heretic does not like a writing which directly or indirectly condemns his or a somewhat similar heresy." See Wm. Hendriksen, *Exposition of the Pastoral Epistles* in his *New Testament Commentary* (Grand Rapids: Baker Book House, 1957), p. 4.

[2]The number of categories varies to some degree in individual writers. Hayes, *Paul and His Epistles* (New York: Methodist Book Concern, 1915), pp. 449-465, lists nine objections and answers each, maintaining Pauline authorship. D. Guthrie, *The Pastoral Epistles* in the *Tyndale New Testament Commentaries* (Grand Rapids: Eerdmans, 1957), pp. 11-52, discusses five major categories, adding "heretical" to the list given above. One of the most thorough and convincing treatments of the whole problem is in Hen-

1. *Historically,* the argument is advanced that these Epistles do not fit into the record of Paul's life as given in the Book of Acts. The most obvious rebuttal is that Acts only records Paul's labors to the end of his two-year Roman imprisonment, but that he was at that time released and continued his ministry for several years longer before his death. References such as I Timothy 1:3 and Titus 1:5 could be fitted in to this last period of his life.[3]

2. *Linguistically,* the number of new words appearing in these Epistles, when compared with the ten other Pauline writings, preclude these from being accepted as genuine.

This argument has been overstressed in many instances.[4] When compared, for example, with the vocabulary of Romans, which few would deny to Paul, the Pastorals do not seem so strikingly different as has been imagined.[5] Positive factors which should be considered here are the subject matter of these Epistles, Paul's increasing vocabulary with the passing of the years, and the versatility of the writer. Such a criterion as a necessarily limited vocabulary would eliminate the "genuine works" of many writers.[6]

---

driksen, *op. cit.,* pp. 4-33. For the denial of Pauline authorship, see Scott, *The Literature of the New Testament* (New York: Morningside Heights, Columbia University Press, 1938), pp. 191-195. It should be added that Scott allows for genuine Pauline fragments within the present Epistles. This is a concession above that of some of the earlier critics.

[3]Guthrie, *op. cit.,* pp. 20, 21, cites both internal and external evidence to support this possibility. It is not necessary to assume that Luke wrote a complete history of Paul's life. See Hayes, *op. cit.,* pp. 462, 463.

[4]A word of caution is added by D. Smith, *The Life and Letters of St. Paul* (London: Hodder & Stoughton, 1919), pp. 582-584. He calls attention to the fact that each of the four groups of the Pauline epistles is marked by linguistic peculiarities. Based on Westcott and Hort's Greek Testament, the four groups contain (1) 6 to 7, (2) 11, (3) 10 to 11 and (4) about 21 peculiarities per page respectively. Thus the Pastorals belong to the Pauline ministry of "a later period, when novel conditions had arisen, new ideas, new problems, new institutions" (p. 584). E. K. Simpson, *The Pastoral Epistles* (Grand Rapids: Eerdmans, 1954), p. 14, adds that a plagiarist would have been careful not to introduce so many new words and thus differ so greatly from the other epistles of Paul.

[5]Hendriksen, *op. cit.,* p. 8 and footnote 5, citing the proportion of new words to total vocabulary, gives the following percentages: Romans, 26.3; II Timothy, 27.6; Titus, 27.6; I Timothy, 32.7. For a list of verbal peculiarities in the Pastorals, see D. Smith, *op. cit.,* pp. 693-696.

[6]"Has any person the right to apply to Paul's writings a criterion which

3. *Doctrinally,* the teachings of these letters are not in accord with the great Pauline emphases of salvation by faith, the believer's union with Christ, the Holy Spirit and the nature of the grace of God. Granted that the modes of expression are not always parallel to the previous ten Epistles and that more emphasis is put upon the proper outworking of salvation rather than its inception, the following passages seem to indicate the same teaching: II Timothy 1:12; II Timothy 1:13; 2:11, 12; Titus 3:5; II Timothy 1:14; Titus 3:7; I Timothy 1:14.

4. *Ecclesiastically,* the organizational features of the Churches are too far advanced for Paul's day and probably indicate an early second century state. This is the "chief argument," says Scott, "that Paul cannot have written the Epistles."[7] The mention of "bishops," "elders" and others is said to preclude a first century date. But this is clearly controverted by a number of considerations: First, the terms "bishop" and "elder" are used interchangeably in Titus 1:5-7; this was not so in the second century. Second, in Acts 6, there is seen a division of responsibility between the apostles and "the Seven." In Acts 14:23, on his first missionary journey, Paul appointed elders in the churches, and there are also officeholders at Ephesus in Acts 20:17, 28.

In addition, the Philippian Epistle was addressed to "the saints . . . with the bishops and deacons" (1:1). Third, the simple requirements set down differ markedly from the more elaborate specifications for officeholders of the second century. These are mainly moral and spiritual characteristics of the elders and deacons; the rise of the episcopate in the second century brought further demands. The enrollment of widows (I Tim. 5) need not be taken in the sense of the establishment of a distinct order. The Pauline authorship may, therefore, be fairly asserted and is in keeping with both external and internal testimony.

---

would do away with much of Milton, Shelley, and Carlyle, if it were applied to their writings?" Hendriksen, *op. cit.,* p. 13. See his detailed discussion of the vocabulary of Titus 2, pp. 377-381. Also Hiebert, *An Introduction to the Pauline Epistles* (Chicago: Moody Press, 1954), pp. 315, 316.

[7]*Op. cit.,* p. 193.

Date and Destination

The date of these Epistles is directly related to the question of Paul's imprisonment. Assuming that Luke's record in Acts ends where it does because there was no more to be said at that point,[8] the theory of Paul's release and subsequent travels becomes both possible and, in the light of the details of the Pastorals, necessary. The apostle, therefore, was free to carry on further missionary endeavor. Further, as I Timothy and Titus give no hint that the Roman government considered Christianity to be a *religio illicita* (illegal religion), as was the case following the Neronian persecution of A.D. 64, these first two letters may be dated about A.D. 63. II Timothy, written just before Paul's death (cf. 4:6 ff.), and showing evidence of official Roman displeasure, is placed at about A.D. 67. Paul's traveling companions are the addressees of each letter.

I TIMOTHY

The first mention of Timothy in the New Testament is in Acts 16:1 ff. Paul, traversing the Galatian cities on his second journey, heard good reports of this young man and took him with them as a member of the missionary party. From this point onward the two worked closely together in the establishment of local churches.

Timothy was Paul's "true child in faith" (I Tim. 1:2). Possibly he was a convert of the apostle on the occasion of Paul's first visit to Lystra and Derbe (Acts 14:6).[9] He was the son of a Greek father and a Jewish mother (Acts 16:1, 3), and had learned "the sacred writings" from his youth (II Tim. 3:14, 15). As a representative of the apostle, he was left at Ephesus to disentangle vexing doctrinal problems and to carry on the organization of the Church (I Tim. 1:3 ff.; 3:1 ff.). Later on, Paul requested him to come to Rome (II Tim. 4:9). Whether he ever made the journey or not is problematical. The writer

---

[8]Tenney, *The New Testament: An Historical and Analytical Survey* (Grand Rapids: Eerdmans, 1953), p. 325.

[9]It is likely that Timothy was a native of Lystra. In Acts 20:4 Luke refers to "Gaius of Derbe, and Timotheus." As Acts 16:1 connects Timothy with the locale of Lystra and Derbe, this reference would seem to point to Lystra rather than Derbe as the place of Timothy's residence.

of Hebrews makes a final reference to Timothy's being "set at liberty" (13:23) and continuing his missionary labors.

Some difficult tasks were assigned to Timothy by Paul, showing the confidence which the apostle placed in this fellow worker (see esp. I Thess. 3:1, 2; I Cor. 4:17; I Tim. 1:3).[10] In the face of his natural timidity,[11] Paul exhorts him to take his stand and maintain the teachings of the Word of God. See especially 4:12-16.

Purpose

To give Timothy personal advice and to instruct him in ecclesiastical matters, Paul wrote this first letter to his companion. The personal exhortations concerned Timothy's attitude toward his work and those about him, and his personal example (4:6-16; 5:1 ff.; 6:11 ff.). Matters relating to the ordering of the church were erroneous teaching (1:3-7, 18-20; 6:3-5), the worship of the Church (2:1-12), the leaders of the church (3:1-13) and their responsibilities (5:17 ff.). Instruction concerning the care of widows was also included (5:3-16).

Outline

The general theme of the book might well be expressed in the words of Paul to Timothy: "Take heed to thyself and to thy teaching" (3:16). Timothy was exhorted to give attention to his own condition and ministry and to exercise care in the organization and guidance of the Ephesian church.

I. Salutation   1:1, 2

II. Charge to Timothy   1:3-20

III. Exhortations for Church Order:
Prayer and Worship   2:1-15

IV. Requirements for Church Officers:
Elders and Deacons   3:1-13

V. Parenthesis   3:14-16

---

[10] Hiebert, *op. cit.*, p. 328.
[11] D. Smith, *op. cit.*, p. 605.

VI. Instructions for Church Activities   4:1—6:21a
   1. In view of prophesied apostasy   4:1-11
   2. In view of private duties   4:12-16
   3. In view of problem situations   5:1—6:10
   4. In view of personal responsibilities   6:11-21a

VII. Conclusion   6:21b

The charge for the responsibility of the Church is laid upon Timothy (1:18) and involves matters of order and organization. Corporate prayer and worship are described briefly by Paul, separate attention being given to the respective duties of men and women (2:1-15).[12] Prayer for " all men" is here enjoined upon believers, political leaders being singled out as special objects of supplication (2:2).

Those who govern the church must be of exemplary character. The requirements for the elders, deacons and "deaconesses"[13] are outlined by Paul in 3:1-13. Among other things, the elder must be "apt to teach" and able to exercise proper authority in the church of God. As one who cares mainly for the material needs of the Church, the deacon must not be "greedy of filthy lucre" (3:8; cf. I Peter 5:2, Titus 1:7, where the same expression is applied to the elder).

The parenthetical section, 3:14-16, is a concise statement of the meaning of the incarnation. It is closely related to the paragraph which follows in that it shows the sanctity of human life (the divine Lord was manifested "in the flesh") and forms the basis for the condemnation of asceticism (4:3-5).

---

[12]The injunction that a woman is neither "to teach, nor to have dominion over a man, but to be in quietness" (2:12) has often been ignored on the one hand, and pressed to the extreme on the other by misinterpretation. Paul's prohibition here relates, not to speaking in general but to the authoritative declaration of doctrine in public services of the church. "The public teacher of God's people does not only tell others what they need to know, but in the capacity of such a teacher he stands before his audience to rule and govern it with the Word." R. C. H. Lenski, *The Interpretation of St. Paul's Epistles to the Colossians, to the Thessalonians, to Timothy, to Titus and to Philemon* (Columbus: Lutheran Book Concern, 1937), p. 574. (Carefully cf. I Cor. 11:2-16; 14:34-36.)

[13]The "women" mentioned here may have been deaconesses in their own right. Note Romans 16:1 where Phoebe is called a "servant," literally, "deaconess." R. C. H. Lenski, *The Interpretation of St. Paul's Epistle to the Romans* (Columbus: Lutheran Book Concern, 1936), states that the terms here indicate "an official position by appointment of the church" and compares the situation here with Acts 6:1-6 (p. 900).

Timothy's responsibilities to various types of people within the Church are clearly outlined in chapters 5 and 6. Respect and purity are always necessary (5:1, 2). Widows are to be cared for if they are elderly and forlorn; others may be assigned to useful positions in the church. Younger widows are encouraged to marry and rear children. The responsibilities of elders are briefly mentioned, together with admonitions to employees and employers (6:1, 2).

"The love of money is the root of all kinds of evil" (6:10), so Paul warns against elevating the desire for material goods above spiritual realities. Rather than having one's hope "set on the uncertainty of riches," let it be "on God, who giveth us richly all things to enjoy" (6:17). So in the face of various kinds of pitfalls, Timothy is exhorted throughout the Epistle to stand firm as a man of God in the service of his Lord.

TITUS

Strange as it may seem, the name of Titus does not appear in the Book of Acts. Of all the major companions of the Apostle, only he and Luke are not mentioned there by name although Luke is included anonymously in the "we sections."

It appears from Galatians 2:1-3 that Titus was a Greek convert of Antioch. Paul calls him "my true child after a common faith" (Titus 1:4). He accompanied Paul and Barnabas to Jerusalem and stood as "Exhibit A of the uncircumcised Gentile believers"[14] before the leaders of the Church. He was sent by Paul to Corinth and apparently succeeded in alleviating the tension there (II Cor. 7:6, 13, 14) and in collecting the money for the poor (II Cor. 8:6, 16, 23). Paul later left him in Crete (Titus 1:5) and, according to the apostle's final letter, he was sent to Dalmatia (II Tim. 4:10).

Purpose

Titus, Paul's "trouble-shooter," was left in Crete to correct disorders in the churches of the island and to appoint elders (1:5). Apparently there was a lack of order in the corporate and individual lives of the Cretan believers. Strong emphasis

---

[14]M. C. Tenney, op. cit., p. 350.

is put upon "good works" in this Epistle, not as a basis of salvation, but as the expression of a proper doctrinal orientation (1:16; 2:7, 14; 3:1, 8, 14; see 3:5).

Outline

The theme of the Epistle is "sound doctrine." Titus embodies a summary of the doctrinal instruction of the early Church as it entered the institutional stage of its growth.[15]

I. Salutation	1:1-4
II. Paul's Instructions to Titus	1:5—3:11
1. Regarding the churches	1:5-16
2. Regarding individuals	2:1-15
3. Regarding the world	3:1-8
4. Regarding heresies	3:9-11
III. Personal Notes	3:12-14
IV. Conclusion	3:15

A summary of the main doctrinal themes of the Epistle contains the following emphases:

1. *The doctrine of God.* He is eternal (1:3), He gives grace and peace (1:4), He has revealed Himself (2:10) and is our Saviour (3:4). Paul is His bondservant (1:1).

2. *The doctrine of Christ.* He is our Saviour (1:4; 2:13; 3:6). Notice that this same title is applied both to God and Christ. The statement in 2:13 is especially significant as a witness to the deity of Christ.[16]

3. *The doctrine of the Holy Spirit.* He is the agent of regeneration (3:5).

4. *The doctrine of the Word of God.* God has manifested

---

[15] *Ibid.,* p. 351.

[16] See the excellent treatment of the passage in Bruce Metzger's "The Jehovah's Witnesses and Jesus Christ" in *Theology Today,* April, 1953. Reprinted by the Theological Book Agency, Princeton, N. J.

His word in the preached message (*kerygma*), and it is to be the standard for life (1:3; 2:5, 10). It is called "faithful" in 1:9 and 3:8. Notice the emphasis on proper teaching of the Word of God (1:9; 2:1, 7, 10). In conjunction with this is the warning against heresy, apparently a Jewish-Gnostic type of teaching (1:10, 14; 3:9).

5. *The doctrine of the (local) church.* The apostle writes with authority (1:1, 3). The requirements for elders are prescribed (1:6-8) together with their duties (1:9). The responsibilities of believers are outlined in 2:1—3:2.[17]

II TIMOTHY

The last words of any great man hold the attention of those who have known of him. The Second Epistle to Timothy constitutes "the last utterance of one of the greatest men that God ever made."[18]

Paul found himself in straitened circumstances as he penned this final letter. While his first imprisonment had been not entirely restrictive (Acts 28:30, 31) and he was able to look forward to his release (Phil. 1:24-26), the second confinement seemed to be the termination of the apostle's earthly ministry (II Tim. 4:6). Only Luke, his faithful physician, was now beside him (4:11); all others, for one reason or another, had left Rome. It was Paul's wish that Timothy would pay him a last visit, and so he writes requesting him to come, bringing Mark with him (4:11).[19]

---

[17]One of the classic doctrinal statements of the New Testament is 2:11-14. It consists of the grace of God in salvation (v. 11), sanctification (v. 12) and expectation (v. 13). Verse 14 tells of the work of Christ in saving, sanctifying and fitting for service.

[18]Scroggie, *The New Testament*, p. 259.

[19]After his early defection (Acts 13:13) which incurred Paul's disfavor (Acts 15:38, 39), Mark had apparently recovered himself, possibly through the efforts of Barnabas, his cousin, and Peter (Col. 4:10; I Peter 5:13).

Purpose

Paul wrote to encourage Timothy as he was about to be left with the heavy burden of the Ephesian church and the sister churches of Asia. He exhorted him to "stir up the gift of God" which was in him (1:6), to endure hardness (1:8), to hold "the pattern of sound words" (1:13), to fulfill his ministry (4:5). Many of the problems which faced the apostle as he wrote I Timothy and Titus appear also in II Timothy but the outlook seems darker (see esp. 1:15; 2:16; 3:12, 13; 4:3, 4). As a part of the personal message of this letter, Paul requests that Timothy visit him shortly (4:9) and bring with him his cloak, books and parchments (4:13).[20]

Outline

As the letter is Paul's final message, it may easily be entitled "An Apostle's Farewell." It is comprised primarily of counsel of a personal nature relating to Timothy's pastoral responsibilities.

I. Salutation	1:1, 2
II. Thanksgiving for Timothy	1:3-18
1. For past blessings	1:3-5
2. For future hardships	1:6-14
3. For present conditions	1:15-18
III. Exhortations to Timothy	2:1-26
1. As a child	2:1, 2
2. As a soldier	2:3, 4
3. As an athlete	2:5
4. As a husbandman	2:6-13
5. As a workman	2:14-19
6. As a vessel	2:20-23
7. As a servant	2:24-26

---

[20]D. Smith, *op. cit.*, p. 635, note 5, suggests that the "books" were likely personal documents of papyrus, while the "parchments" were vellum rolls containing the Old Testament Scriptures. On this request of the apostle as compared to William Tyndale's letter from his prison cell, see F. F. Bruce, *The Books and the Parchments* (London: Pickering & Inglis, Ltd., 1953), p. 9.

IV. Warnings to Timothy   3:1-17
   1. In view of (the) last days   3:1-13
   2. In the light of past learning   3:14-17

 V. The Final Charge to Timothy   4:1-8
   1. The serious responsibilities   4:1-5
   2. The apostolic example   4:6-8

VI. Personal Instructions to Timothy   4:9-21

VII. Conclusion   4:22

The special features of II Timothy are mainly three: 1) The sevenfold portrayal of the believer in chapter 2. By means of these seven common figures Paul exhorts Timothy to fulfill all that is expected of him. 2) The declaration concerning the nature of the Scriptures in 3:14-17. They are described as "the sacred writings" and the "scripture" and are declared to be "inspired of God." The knowledge of the Word of God was to be a guardian against evil men and apostasy. 3) The final charge to Timothy in 4:1-8. Not only is Timothy faced with a solemn task, but Paul points to his own ministry as a pattern (4:7, 8).

The Value of the Pastoral Epistles

Tenney[21] has sketched three tendencies which should be noted by all who read these letters:

1. Heresy is continuing to progress and constitutes a serious menace to even the youngest in the ministry.

2. A greater stress is thereby laid upon more creedal formulation than is evident in the earlier Epistles. Such phrases as "hold the form of sound words," the formula "faithful is the saying," and the phrase "sound doctrine" all point to statements of principle in the growing Church.

3. While the Church was realizing its institutional phase, it was not "a fixed hierarchy or a machine organization." Spiritual vitality and the missionary motive were still evident.

A Final Tribute

The keen analysis by D. A. Hayes of the character of Paul

---
[21]*Op. cit.*, pp. 354, 355.

as seen in his epistles is quoted here as a final tribute to the greatest leader of the first or possibly any century of the Church's history:

"In First and Second Thessalonians we studied Paul the preacher and apocalyptic seer and we came to understand something of the methods of his ministry and the meanings of his prophecy. In First and Second Corinthians we studied Paul the pastor and the apolgete, the unparalleled organizer of churches and the undaunted defender of his Christian experience and faith. In the Epistles to the Galatians and to the Romans we studied Paul the protestant against all restrictions of religious liberty in thought and in life and Paul the professor of theology, systematizing for all time to come the doctrines of redemption and salvation from sin. In the Prison Epistles we found a picture of Paul the personal friend of Onesimus and Philemon and the Philippians and the inspired idealist of the identification of the individual Christian with Christ and of Christ with the universal church. In the Pastoral Epistles we rejoiced to find another glimpse of the consistent and confident and cheerful and courageous veteran of the many victorious battlefields, facing now towards his eternal sainthood in heaven."[22]

Suggested Readings

Bernard, J. H. The Pastoral Epistles in the Cambridge Greek Testament. Cambridge: The University Press, 1922.

Fairbairn, P. Commentary on the Pastoral Epistles. Grand Rapids: Zondervan Publishing House, 1956 (reprint).

Guthrie, D. The Pastoral Epistles in the Tyndale New Testament Commentaries. Grand Rapids: Wm. B. Eerdmans Publishing Co., 1957.

Hendriksen, W. Exposition of the Pastoral Epistles in New Testament Commentary. Grand Rapids: Baker Book House, 1957.

Kent, H. A. The Pastoral Epistles. Chicago: Moody Press, 1958.

King, G. H. A Leader Led: An Expositional Study of I Timothy. London: Marshall, Morgan and Scott, 1951. Rich devotional studies.

King, G. H. To My Son: An Expositional Study of II Timothy. London: Marshall, Morgan and Scott, 1944. Rich devotional studies.

Simpson, E. K. The Pastoral Epistles. Grand Rapids: Wm. B. Eerdmans Publishing Co., 1954. Based on Greek text.

---

[22]Op. cit., pp. 486, 487.

CHAPTER 13

THE JEWISH-CHRISTIAN EPISTLES: HEBREWS AND JAMES

Introduction

THE FACT that these Epistles were written primarily to converts from Judaism sets them apart from the remaining New Testament letters. This conclusion is assumed from the content of Hebrews (see esp. 1:1; 8:13, etc.), while James specifically identifies his audience (1:1). Both books have a marked Old Testament orientation. Hebrews dwells upon the history of Israel, the priesthood and the Tabernacle. James employs the proverbial style of the Wisdom literature and uses common Old Testament phrases such as those found in 1:10, 19; 3:9; 4:6; 5:4, 11. In addition, James contains many parallels with the Sermon on the Mount.[1]

HEBREWS

Authorship

Before proceeding further, attention should be given to the chief problem of the Epistle. This is the question of authorship. As will be readily noticed, the book is anonymous. Outside of I, II and III John, this is the only New Testament Epistle in which the author's name is omitted from the letter itself.

Historically, Hebrews was anonymous in the early years of the Church, even in Alexandria where Paul's name became connected with it by the end of the second century. In the Western church, the Pauline tradition was asserted in the fourth century and generally accepted by the fifth century.

---

[1]Scroggie, *Know Your Bible: The New Testament*, Vol. II. (London: Pickering & Inglis, Ltd., n.d.), p. 297, lists fifteen passages in the Epistle which contain reflections of Jesus' teaching in Matthew 5-7.

Tertullian, in North Africa, defended the name of Barnabas as the writer. In the sixteenth century, Martin Luther ascribed it to Apollos and this view became increasingly popular with present-day scholars. Farrar, in the *Cambridge Greek Testament*,[2] defends this position, citing eleven facts concerning the writer as indicated by the Epistle itself and concludes that either Apollos or an entirely unknown person wrote the Epistle. Perhaps the present state of knowledge has not advanced much beyond Origen who, in the third century, stated that "Who it was who wrote the Epistle, God alone knows certainly."[3]

While the doctrine of the Epistle is Pauline and the reference to Timothy in 13:23 may link it with Paul, the style and language of the book, together with the statement in 2:3, seems to oppose such a conclusion.[4] The style of the book is polished; the Greek more nearly approaches the classical style than any other New Testament books except Luke and Acts.[5] Only the Septuagint (Greek) version of the Old Testament is used in quotations; Paul frequently quoted from the Hebrew text and his formula of quotation also differs. The viewpoint of Hebrews concerning the Law is that it is a "shadow" (10:1) or a "figure" (9:9); Paul spoke of the Law as bearing a "curse" (Gal. 3:13) and holding people in bondage (Gal. 5:1). It may be said, therefore, that if Paul was the author the differences in style and language must be looked at in the light of the subject matter, destination and purpose, and not *vice versa*.

---

[2]Pp. lv-lvii.

[3]Moffatt, *The Epistle to the Hebrews* in the *International Critical Commentary* (Edinburgh: T. & T. Clark, 1924) says, "Perhaps our modern pride resents being baffled by an ancient document, but it is better to admit that we are not yet wiser on this matter than Origen was, seventeen centuries ago" (p. xx). A convenient survey of the problem in the early church is given by T. Rees, "Epistle to the Hebrews" in the *International Standard Bible Encyclopedia* (Grand Rapids: Eerdmans, rev. ed., 1939), II, 1356, 1357.

[4]This reference should be compared with Galatians 1:1, 12, where Paul emphatically affirms that his message was by direct "revelation of Jesus Christ." The writer of Hebrews states that his message "was confirmed unto us by them that heard."

[5]Clement of Alexandria A.D. 200, in fact, suggested that Luke himself wrote out the Greek translation of Paul's Hebrew Epistle.

Date and Destination

The Epistle cannot be later than about A.D. 80 or 90 as Clement of Rome quoted from it in A.D. 95.[6] Those who date it shortly before the fall of the Temple in A.D. 70[7] usually refer to the following passages to substantiate an earlier dating: 1) the allusion to continuing sacrifices (10:11); 2) the nearness of persecution (10:32-36; 12:4); 3) the liberation and ministry of Timothy (13:23).

If the authorship of the Epistle is a difficult problem, the original destination is even more obscure.[8] First, who were the readers? Second, where were they located? It has generally been assumed that they were a Jewish audience, converted to Christianity or at least professing to believe in Christ. While the readers are nowhere identified precisely, the many references to Judaism and the rituals of the Old Testament (1:1; 2:16; 3:9; 8:13; 9:1; 13:13) may be taken as indications of a Jewish readership. But it must remain a position based on the epistle as a whole rather than any specific references in the book. These readers may have been located in Rome (cf. 13: 24, "They of Italy salute you") or in Palestine.[9] The phrase "of Italy" may be understood in one of two ways: (1) of persons residing in Italy (if the letter was written in Rome) who were sending their greetings to friends in some other place; or, (2) of persons who had come "from" Italy and were sending greetings back to their homeland.

Purpose

Solemn warnings are scattered throughout this book. They

---

[6]Scott places it "somewhere between 80 and 90 A.D." He mentions that many date it before A.D. 70 but feels that "it reflects a type of Christian thinking which belongs to the later part of the century." *The Literature of the New Testament* (New York: Morningside Heights: Columbia University Press, 1938), p. 199.

[7]So Tenney, *The New Testament*, p. 374; Scroggie, *op. cit.*, pp. 266, 267; Manley, *New Bible Handbook*, p. 390.

[8]Rees, *op. cit.*, p. 1358. Scott, *op. cit.*, p. 199, considers it the crucial question as it determines our understanding of the purpose of the Epistle.

[9]See B. F. Westcott, *The Epistle to the Hebrews* (Grand Rapids: Wm. B. Eerdmans, 1951), pp. xv-lxxxiv, for a full discussion of introductory problems.

are addressed to the Jewish Christian readers who were evidently failing to progress in their Christian experience. The writer, therefore, exhorts them to appropriate by faith the blessings of salvation and not to stop short of the spiritual rest which God has provided (4:1).

Accompanying this note is the emphasis on the superiority of Christ and the finality of Christianity.[10] The key word of the Epistle is "better," occurring thirteen times (1:4; 6:9; 7:7, 19, 22; 8:6, twice; 9:23; 10:34; 11:16, 35, 40; 12:24). A note of finality is added by the use of the words "perfect," "eternal" (or "forever") and the expression "once for all" (7:27; 9:12; 10:10).

Outline

Unlike the books which have preceded it, Hebrews has no introductory statement. It plunges immediately into the consideration of its chief subject.

I. The Superiority of Christ	1:1—10:18
1. Above the prophets	1:1-3
2. Above the angels	1:4-14; 2:5-18
First warning: neglect	2:1-4
3. Above Moses	3:1-6
Second warning: unbelief	3:7-19
4. Above Joshua	4:2-10
Third warning: unbelief	4:1, 11-13
5. Above Aaron	4:14—5:10
Fourth warning: immaturity	5:11—6:20
6. Above the Levitical Priesthood	7:1-28
7. Above the Old Covenant	8:1-13
8. Above the Ordinances and Sacrifices	9:1—10:18
II. The Superiority of Faith	10:19—13:21
1. The way of access to God	10:19-25

[10]J. B. Green, in "Christianity: the Ultimate Religion," *Christianity Today,* Volume IV, number 21, July 20, 1959, pp. 3-5, cites three things showing Christianity to be the perfect religion: (1) It perfectly reveals God; (2) it takes away sin; (3) it perfectly reconciles God and man.

Fifth warning: willful sin	10:26-31
2. The way of life in the world	10:32—11:40
3. The way of training as sons of God	12:1-13
Sixth warning: apostasy	12:14-17
4. The way of heavenly privilege	12:18-24
Seventh warning: refusal	12:25-29
5. The way of duty among men	13:1-21
III. Conclusion and Greetings	13:22-25

The author of the Epistle writes in bold contrasts: the partial and the complete; the old and the new; the temporal and the eternal; immaturity and maturity; the imperfect and the perfect; the temporary and the final.

His argument has both a positive and a negative aspect. The positive aspect is that Christ is superior to all persons and priestly institutions of Old Testament days.

1. The Son is superior to the sages	1:1-3
2. The Creator is superior to the creature	1:4—2:18
3. The Master is superior to the servants	3:1—4:13
4. The Great High Priest is superior to the Levitcal priests	4:14—7:28
5. The New Covenant is superior to the Old Covenant	8:1-13
6. The Sinless Sacrifice is superior to animal sacrifices	9:1—10:18

The negative aspect is that because there is danger in the Christian's slipping away from the place of privilege and responsibility into which God has placed him, he must beware and continue to make progress. To enforce the thought the writer constantly uses the hortatory expression, "Let us." The most important are listed below:

1. Let us fear	4:1
2. Let us give diligence	4:11
3. Let us hold fast our confession	4:14
4. Let us draw near	4:16

5. Let us be carried along unto perfection[11]   6:1
6. Let us draw near   10:22
7. Let us hold fast the confession   10:23
8. Let us consider one another   10:24
9. Let us lay aside every weight   12:1
10. Let us run with patience   12:1
11. Let us have grace   12:28
12. Let us go forth unto Him   13:13
13. Let us offer up a sacrifice of praise   13:15

In 4:1 and 6:1 the whole hortatory design is epitomized: "let us fear" and "let us be carried along unto perfection."

The opening verses of the book declare first, the *concept* of revelation: "God hath spoken." In the Old Testament times the Word came in many parts and in many ways through the prophets. As the mouthpiece of God, the prophet declared His will for man (Exod. 4:10-12; 7:1, 2). Now the climax has come—God has spoken in His Son.

Next, the *character* of revelation is delineated. Both in time past and in the end of days it was God who spoke. This is a consistent witness. Truly amazing is the unity of the Scriptures as the message comes through more than 40 human writers and spans a period of 1,500 years.

Finally, the *channel* of revelation is denoted. First it was the voice of the prophets; then it was the voice of the Son. One was preliminary, the other final. In 1:2, 3 the writer gives a sevenfold description of the Son, showing His superiority to the prophets in relation to God, the world and mankind.

When describing the relationship of Christ to the angelic beings, the writer shows Him as vastly superior primarily because He is their Creator (1:10), He receives their worship (1:6), and He is the Son while they are God's servants (1:5, 7, 8, 14). Only temporarily, for the purposes of redemption, was

---

[11]The Greek verb in 6:1 is in the passive, rather than the active or middle voice. The stress here is upon the idea that God's power is available to bring the believer to maturity; he must yield himself to its active influence.

He made "lower than the angels" (2:9). Following His death He was "crowned with glory and honor" (2:9).[12]

Christ is superior to Moses as the Builder of the house is above the servant in the house (3:1-6). Neither Moses nor Joshua (4:8) could bring real rest to the people of God. Their labors, at best, were imperfect copies of the true spiritual rest which is found in Christ.

The heart of the Epistle deals with the High Priesthood of Christ and the superiority of His person and work to that of the Levitical priests and institutions (4:14—10:18). By means of a series of contrasts with the Old Testament priests and ordinances, the truth of His position is made clear.

Christ	*Old Testament Order*
a great high priest 4:14	a high priest 5:1
after the order of Melchizedek 5:10	after order of Aaron 7:11
an endless life 7:16	subject to death 7:23
surety of a better covenant 7:22	weak and unprofitable 7:18
unchangeable priesthood 7:24	constant change 7:23
able to save to uttermost 7:25	hindered from continuing 7:23
sinless and perfected 7:26, 28	sinful and imperfect 7:27, 28
at right hand of the Majesty in the heavens 8:1	served in earthly place 8:5
a minister of the true tabernacle 8:2; 9:24	served in man-made center 8:2; 9:24
a mediator of a better covenant 8:6	old and aged covenant 8:13
obtained eternal redemption 9:12	temporary measure 9:9, 10
cleansed the conscience 9:14	cleansed the flesh 9:13
put away sin once for all 9:26	yearly sacrifices for sin 9:25
obtained sanctification once for all 10:10	sacrifices could not take away sins 10:11

---

[12]Cf. Philippians 2:6-11; John 17:5, 24.

In the final major division of the Epistle (10:19—13:21), great stress is put upon the superiority of faith as contrasted with works. Not only must a person be justified by faith but he must then walk by faith. The writer reminds his readers of their beginning (10:32) and exhorts them to press on in faith rather than being like those who "shrink back unto perdition" (10:39). Chapter 11 is the great gallery of Old Testament heroes of faith; chapter 12 exhorts, "Let us also . . . run with patience the race that is set before us" (12:1). To bring the believer to maturity, the Father chastises when necessary (12: 7-10). This maturity is to be evidenced in the divine way of life (13:1-17). These great heavenly truths are to be seen in action in the earthly circumstances of the children of faith.

JAMES

Introduction

The outlook of Jewish writers, as may be clearly seen in the Old Testament books, was primarily practical and ethical. Religion was not a matter of theory and speculation, as in pagan cultures, but of revealed truth which was intended to be the guide for the life of the individual. The Epistle of James fits into this category. The book emphasizes duty rather than doctrine. Except for two occurrences of the name of Christ (1:1; 2:1) and the reference to "the coming [parousia] of the Lord" (5:7), this letter might as properly fit into the Old Testament as the New.

Author

At the outset the writer identifies himself as "James, a servant of God and of the Lord Jesus Christ" (1:1).[13] In the New Testament there are at least four men by this name. The brother of John and son of Zebedee was called James (Matt. 4:21). He was killed early in the history of the Church, falling victim to the rage of Herod Agrippa I (Acts 12:1, 2). Another of the disciples of Jesus bore the same name (Matt. 10:3, "the son of Alphaeus"). There was a James who was the father of

---

[13]See Jude 1 where the writer describes himself as "Jude, a servant of Jesus Christ, and brother of James."

another of Jesus' disciples (Luke 6:16, Judas, not Iscariot). Finally, there was James who was the brother of Jesus (Matt. 13:55), being one of the four brothers of our Lord.

Traditionally, the Church has linked the writer of this Epistle with "James, the Lord's brother."[14] He appears in the New Testament (aside from the Synoptic Gospels) in John 7:3-5, where he is evidently an unbeliever; in I Corinthians 15:7, as one to whom the resurrected Christ appears; in Acts 1:14, along with his mother and brothers at the Jerusalem prayer meeting; and in Acts 12:17; 15:13-29; 21:18; and Galatians 2:9 where he emerges as a leader in the Jerusalem church. The Jewish character of this epistle is in keeping with the character of James as he appears in Acts and Galatians. He is "the apostle of good works."[15]

One further word may be added regarding the position of this Epistle in the Church. It was slow in being universally recognized as part of the New Testament Canon. The Eastern churches (Jerusalem and Antioch) acknowledged it earlier than those in the West (Rome and Carthage). At the Council of Carthage in A.D. 397 it attained acceptance in the West, was universally acknowledged at Chalcedon in A.D. 451, and was then secure until the days of the Reformation when Luther inveighed against it, calling it a "downright strawy Epistle."

Date and Destination

Decisive proof is not apparent for any definite date. By many it is considered to be the earliest New Testament writing, and is thus dated at about A.D. 45. This early date for the Epistle is probable because of its reflection of a Judaic Christianity which is basically concerned with moral principles rather than the problems and controversies of the next decade or two. Others

---

[14]At least three views have been held as to the meaning of the term "brother": 1) the natural sense, that this man was the child of Joseph and Mary. This would make Jesus older than James; 2) the sense of "stepbrother," which states that this man was a son of Joseph by a former marriage, and therefore older than Jesus; 3) the sense of "cousin," which understands the word to mean that this James was the son of Alphaeus and Mary, a sister of Mary the mother of Jesus.

[15]See further, Tenney, op. cit., pp. 276, 277.

however, place it near the end of James's life, early in the sixties of the first century.

The address of the letter is "to the twelve tribes which are of the Dispersion" (1:1). James writes to fellow Jews, believers in Christ. Not infrequently in Jewish history, though particularly in 721 and 586 B.C.,[16] the people found themselves scattered, taken as captives to foreign lands. Others had left Palestine in the interests of commercial ventures in various parts of the Roman Empire. On the day of Pentecost, as recorded in Acts 2:9-11, Jews from all parts of the ancient world had come to Jerusalem to be in attendance at the Feast. Doubtless as a result of the response to Peter's message (2:41) the Gospel went out all across the Empire with the returning pilgrims. In addition, Christians from the Jerusalem Church being "scattered abroad went about preaching the word" (Acts 8:4).

Purpose

James writes this letter to analyze the nature of genuine faith and to urge his readers to demonstrate the validity of their trust in Christ. While doctrinal truths underlie his argument, James stresses the duties of the believer. The whole position is summed up in one crisp sentence: "But be ye doers of the word, and not hearers only, deluding your own selves" (1:22). To James, a "doer" is one who possesses true faith and expresses it in every area of life.

Outline

I. Introduction		1:1
II. The Test of Faith		1:2-27
1. Facing temptation		1:2-18
2. Expressing religion		1:19-27
III. The Nature of Faith		2:1—3:12
1. Regarding the respect of persons		2:1-13

---

[16]In 721 B.C., the nation of Israel was carried into captivity by the Assyrians; in 586 B.C. the kingdom of Judah shared a similar fate under the Babylonians. As less than 50,000 people returned to Judea under Zerubbabel (Ezra 2:64, 65), most of the people stayed in foreign lands. In the 4th century B.C., Alexander the Great transported a number of Jews into Egypt and settled them in Alexandria. In the first century, colonies of Jews were found in most of the cities of the Roman world, especially the commercial centers (Antioch of Syria, Ephesus, Corinth, etc.).

2. Regarding the relation of faith and works   2:14-26
3. Regarding the use of the tongue   3:1-12

IV. The Works of Faith   3:13—4:12
  1. Guided by heavenly wisdom   3:13-18
  2. Characterized by subjection to God   4:1-10
  3. Based on just relationships   4:11, 12

V. The Application of Faith   4:13—5:20
  1. Regarding commercial ventures   4:13-17
  2. Regarding riches   5:1-6
  3. Regarding the coming of the Lord   5:7-11
  4. Regarding oaths   5:12
  5. Regarding prayer   5:13-18
  6. Regarding an erring brother   5:19, 20

James wrote with authority. There is no evidence of apology for what he had to say. His pronouncements carry the weight of an absolute position.

True faith is not injured by temptation. The proof of faith through trials brings added endurance and maturity of character (1:3, 4) and holds the promise of "the crown of life" (1:12). A penetrating analysis of temptation and its relation to sin accompanies these exhortations. Temptation does not come from God (1:13) but originates within the individual (1:14). Four steps characterize the nature of temptation:

1. It *allures* the individual, appealing to his own desires (1:14).

2. It *entices* the individual, as a bait ensnares a fish or an animal (1:14).

3. It *conceives* within the individual, and brings sin to the birth in his life (1:15).

4. As full-grown sin, it *eventuates* in death, separation from God (1:15).

The discussion of the relation of faith and works (2:14-26) is one of the classic passages on the subject to be found in the Bible. This strong argument led Luther to question the propriety of James' place in the Canon. On the surface he seems to contradict what Paul says about faith and works in Romans 4. But what point is James making? The crux of the matter is found in 2:14: "What doth it profit, my brethren, if a man say that he hath faith, but have not works? can that faith save him?" The "faith" of which James speaks is only a *professed* faith, barren of expression. That kind of faith[17] will save no one because it is not true faith. Said Calvin, "Faith alone saves, but the faith which saves is never alone!" True faith in God saved Abraham (Rom. 4:3, 5); that faith showed itself gen-uine in his works (James 2:21-23). The two are, therefore, complementary.[18]

Finally, it may be said that the practical wisdom of James is unsurpassed in the New Testament Epistles. Notice especially the teaching on the nature and use of the tongue (3:1-12); the recognition of the nature of life (4:13-17) and the vital nature of prayer (5:13-18).

Suggested Readings

HEBREWS

Lang, G. H. *The Epistle to the Hebrews.* London: The Paternoster Press, 1951.

Lenski, R. C. H. *Interpretation of the Epistles to the Hebrews and of the Epistle of James.* Columbus: Lutheran Book Concern, 1938. Ex-cellent treatment.

Murray, A. *The Holiest of All.* New York: Fleming H. Revell Co., n.d.

Sauer, E. *In the Arena of Faith.* Grand Rapids: Wm. B. Eerdmans Publishing Co., 1955. Studies in Hebrews 12.

Thomas, W. H. G. *Let Us Go On.* Grand Rapids: Zondervan Publish-ing House, 1944.

---

[17]"James here speaks of faith, not in general, but in particular. It is a *certain kind of* faith; that which the person only *says* he has but does not really possess. The translation in 2:14 in the A.S.V. brings this out clearly, rendering the Greek definite article as "that."

[18]"Lenski, in *The Interpretation of the Epistle to the Hebrews and of the Epistle of James* (Columbus: Lutheran Book Concern, 1938), has stated it concisely: "Paul deals with law-works, which have nothing to do with true Gospel-faith . . . James deals with Gospel-works, which ever evidence the presence of Gospel-faith. . . . " (p. 587)

Westcott, B. F. *The Epistle to the Hebrews.* Grand Rapids: Wm. B. Eerdmans Publishing Co., 1951. The standard work on the Greek text of the epistle.

JAMES

Hayes, D. A. "Epistle of James" in *The International Standard Bible Encyclopedia.* Grand Rapids: Wm. B. Eerdmans Publishing Co., 1939. Volume III, pp. 1562-1567.

King, G. H. *A Belief That Behaves.* London: Marshall, Morgan & Scott, Ltd., n.d. Practical expositions.

Mayor, J. B. *The Epistle of St. James.* Grand Rapids: Zondervan Publishing House, 1955. Detailed introduction and commentary on the Greek text. For the advanced student.

Moorehead, W. G .*Outline Studies in the New Testament: the Catholic Epistles.* New York: Fleming H. Revell Co., 1910.

Strauss, L. *James, Your Brother.* New York: Loizeaux Brothers, 1956.

CHAPTER 14

GENERAL AND PERSONAL EPISTLES: PETER—JUDE

Introduction

THE REMAINING EPISTLES of the New Testament may be classified as *general* (I and II Peter; I John; Jude) and *personal* (II and III John).[1] The former classification indicates that they are not addressed to any particular church; the latter that they are addressed to individuals. Three of the six are anonymous but have been traditionally ascribed to John the apostle. Peter, the writer of two of the books, was a leader in the early Church (Gal. 2:9) while Jude was known as one of the brothers of the Lord and of James (Matt. 13:55).

I PETER

Author

Simon, impulsive and changeable in nature, was called from his trade as a fisherman to be "a fisher of men." On three occasions Jesus called him. The first time he was given a *new name* (John 1:40-42). Jesus stated that the day would come when he would be known as Cephas, or Peter, a rock. This was a prophecy of the change of life which would render him stable and dependable. When the second call came, *new associations* were specified (Luke 5:1-11). Not fish, but men were to be the objects of his energies. Finally, a *new vocation* was realized in Simon's life (Mark 3:13-16). Jesus called him so that he "might be with him" and to send him out "to preach, and to have authority to cast out demons."

Though Peter was intensely loyal to Jesus, his intentions

---

[1]James usually is included under the *general* heading but has been treated along with Hebrews as a Jewish-Christian Epistle (chapter 13).

were often beyond his actual accomplishments. While affirming that he would defend his Lord and even die for Him, it was only a short time until he denied that he even knew Him (Luke 22: 31:34; John 13:36-38; 18:15-27). Following Peter's repentance Jesus restored him to an active service (John 21:15-19).

Together with James and John, the sons of Zebedee, Peter occupied a favored place among the disciples of Jesus. On three recorded occasions these three alone were permitted to be with Jesus at some important happening: at the raising of Jairus' daughter (Luke 8:51), at the Transfiguration scene (Luke 9: 28) and in the Garden of Gethsemane (Matthew 26:37). In the Book of Acts, Peter virtually occupies the central place in most of the first twelve chapters. His leadership, his sermons and his defenses are all noteworthy. According to tradition he was martyred in Rome late in the reign of Nero.

The attestation of the epistle is "widespread, early and clear,"[2] and this external testimony is paralleled by the contents of the book itself. The writer identifies himself as "Peter, an apostle of Jesus Christ" (1:1) and "a fellow-elder, and a witness of the sufferings of Christ" (5:1). Associated with him as he writes are Silvanus (probably Silas, Paul's associate) and Mark (5:12, 13). The frequent references to the Shepherd and the care of the flock is reminiscent of the conversation which Jesus held with Peter in John 21:15-18.

Date and Destination

A date of about A.D. 63-65 would fit the circumstances of the Epistle, and this is the traditional dating. This was the period of Nero's persecution of the Christians in Rome (A.D. 64) and might account for the reference to the impending "fiery trial" which is alluded to in 4:12. If the provincial governors followed the Emperor's example, persecution might well have been felt in Asia Minor as well.

The book is addressed to Christians in a number of the northern provinces in Asia Minor: Pontus, Galatia, Cappodocia, Asia and Bithynia. While it has been assumed that these people were

[2]E. G. Selwyn, *The First Epistle of St. Peter* (London: Macmillan, 1947), p. 38.

Jewish Christians (sojourners of the Dispersion), some of the expressions in the Epistle might as well have reference to Gentile believers (cf. 2:18 ff.; 4:3-5).

Purpose

Peter writes this letter to give hope in the midst of suffering. While the chief word of the Epistle is "suffering," occurring seventeen times,[3] the references to "hope," occurring five times,[4] give the proper perspective in the midst of suffering. In addition, the letter was designed to teach believers to exercise obedience and patience in whatever circumstances they found themselves (2:13-17, 20).

Outline

I. Salutation	1:1, 2
II. Perspective and Suffering	1:3—2:10
1. The hope of the Second Coming	1:3-12
2. The reality of the new life	1:13-25
3. The duties of the new position	2:1-10
III. Pressure and Suffering	2:11—4:6
1. The pressure of desires	2:11, 12
2. The pressure of ordinances	2:13-17
3. The pressure of domestic duties	2:18—3:7
4. The pressure of social relationships	3:8-12
5. The pressure of the world	3:13—4:6
IV. Service and Suffering	4:7-11
V. Witness and Suffering	4:12-19
VI. Personal Attitudes and Suffering	5:1-11
1. The attitudes of elders	5:1-4
2. The attitudes of younger men	5:5a
3. The attitudes of all believers	5:5b-11
VII. Conclusion	5:12-14

[3] It is used of the sufferings of Christ seven times (1:11; 2:21, 23; 3:18; 4:1, 13; 5:11) and of Christians ten times (2:19, 20; 3:14, 17; 4:1, 13, 15, 19; 5:9, 10).
[4] 1:3, 13, 21; 3:5, 15.

Paul wrote to Timothy that "all that would live godly in Christ Jesus shall suffer persecution" (II Tim. 3:12). Peter's Epistle, too, seems to teach that this is the common lot of the believer (2:21). In view of suffering, what is to be the attitude of the believer? At least three answers are suggested by the Epistle.

1. It is to be borne patiently for the sake of Christ, as it was His lot before ours (2:20-24).
2. It is intended to produce positive effects in the Christian life (5:10).
3. It is to be viewed in the light of the second coming (1:7, 13; 4:13).

Further, the apostle stresses the effects of suffering when it is properly borne by the Christian.

1. It affords opportunity for an apologetic for the faith—the readiness to answer those who ask a reason of the hope which we possess (3:13-16).
2. It has a purifying influence (3:17-22).
3. It should produce an alertness in the face of sin around us and the approach of the end of all things (4:1-11).

Another outstanding emphasis of the Epistle is the doctrine of grace.[5] Five of the ten occurrences of the word are linked with God. In 5:10, grace is an attribute of God or an expression of His character. In 4:10; 5:5, 12 and implied in 3:7, grace is given by God to the believer. Grace is also an attitude of God toward those who suffer for His sake (2:19, 20). God's grace, too, is manifold in its nature (4:10).

II PETER

This Epistle, along with the four which follow, is directed against false teachings which were afflicting the churches. The second chapter in particular is similar in nature to the warnings

---

[5] 1:2, 10, 13; 2:19, 20; 3:7; 4:10; 5:5, 10, 12. In 2:19, 20 the word is translated as "acceptable." In addition, the "gift" referred to in 4:10 is a "gracious" gift, or a "gift of grace."

of Paul, John and Jude.[6] These false teachings may well have been the seeds from which the heresies of the second century grew. The denials of the true humanity of the Lord Jesus (I John 4:2), of His Sonship (I John 2:22, 23), of His redemptive work (II Peter 2:1), of His second coming (II Peter 3:4) and even of His Lordship (Jude 4) appeared also in later days in more developed form.

Author

No New Testament book was less readily received by the early Church than II Peter. Critics today almost unanimously reject it as Petrine, or are at least dubious as to its genuineness. Because the letter is brief and lacks the mention of any specific destination, many have classed it as a late work, not written by Peter at all. But it was accepted as canonical by the Church Councils of the fourth century (Laodicea in A.D. 363 and Carthage in A.D. 397) and this fact should not be lightly discounted.

The internal evidence for Petrine authorship, on the other hand, is strong. In his address the writer calls himself "Simon [or, Simeon] Peter, a servant and an apostle of Jesus Christ" (1:1). A forger likely would have followed the style of I Peter 1:1. He testifies to his association with Christ on the Mount of Transfiguration (1:16-18). His affection for Paul is referred to in 3:15, 16. The use of the word "enticing" (2:14, 18), which means "to set a bait," may be a reminiscence of Peter's life as a fisherman. In addition, the idea that a forger would refer to himself and his readers as those who "have obtained a like precious faith" (1:1) and would exhort them to be characterized by "holy living and godliness" (3:11) seems incongruous. Such a hypocrite would hardly escape detection in the early Church.

Date and Destination

Peter was martyred late in Nero's reign, probably A.D. 67 or 68. If his second Epistle was written after the first, it probably

---

[6]Paul warned the Ephesian elders of false teachers (Acts 20:29, 30); he also wrote to the Thessalonians (II Thess. 2:1-3), and Timothy (I Tim. 4:1 ff.; II Tim. 3:1 ff.) about the same matter. (See also I John 2:18-29; II John 7, 9-11; Jude 4-16.)

should be dated between 65 and 67. Some writers, however, place this book before I Peter, dating it early in the sixties.[7]

The recipients of the Epistle are not specified as in I Peter. If II Peter 3:1 is interpreted as referring to the First Epistle, then the destination is the same. Otherwise, it is unknown.

Purpose

Peter wrote this Epistle to re-emphasize certain basic matters. The word "remember" occurs in three places (1:12, 13; 3:1) and its companion "forget" in two places (1:9; 3:8). His readers were to remember that the Word of God was normative for them and that the hope of the second coming must not be destroyed by false teaching . There is a call to go on in their Christian experience (1:3-11) and to live in a holy and godly manner (3:11).

Outline

The key word is "knowledge" (lit., "full knowledge") and occurs in 1:2, 3, 5, 6, 8, 16, 20; 2:20, 21; 3:3, 17, 18. Proper knowledge of the Lord and His Word is the antidote to false teaching and improper living.

I. Introduction	1:1, 2
II. Knowledge and the Christian Life	1:3-11
1. The divine provision	1:3, 4
2. The believer's responsibility	1:5-11
III. Knowledge and the Word of God	1:12-21
1. The experience of the apostles	1:12-18
2. The message of the prophets	1:19-21
IV. Knowledge and the False Teaching	2:1-22
1. Description of the false teachers	2:1-3
2. Judgment of the false teachers	2:4-19

---

[7]Lenski, *The Interpretation of the Epistles of St. Peter, St. John and St. Jude* (Columbus: Lutheran Book Concern, 1938), pp. 241, 242. He observes that in the New Testament the longest Epistles are placed first, the shortest last, irrespective of the date of writing. Such is the case with Paul's epistles and John's along with Peter's. The reference in II Peter 3:1 is taken to be a reference to a lost letter, not I Peter. (Cf. the case in I Cor. 5:9.)

3. Danger of the false teaching   2:20-22

V. Knowledge and the Second Coming   3:1-13
   1. The mockers and their error   3:1-7
   2. The day and its character   3:8-13

VI. Conclusion: Steadfastness and Growth   3:14-18

Two passages of special interest in the Epistle are 1:19-21 and 3:8-13, the former dealing with the nature of the Scriptures, the latter relating to the coming of the day of the Lord. Peter emphasizes that the Holy Spirit is the true source of the message of the prophets (1:21) and that because of the unity of the Word of God any single passage must be taken as a part of the total context. Rather than discouraging personal interpretation it stresses the proper means of understanding the Scriptures.[8]

In the face of the denials of the second advent (1:4), the apostle affirms the certainty of the coming of the Day of the Lord. As the earth was once inundated as a sign of the judgment of God (3:6), so again will He act, this time by fire (3:10). Only God's longsuffering postpones the final judgment (3:9). Such an expectation should produce "holy living and godliness" on the part of the believer (3:11).

I JOHN

Background

As the Gospel and the First Epistle of John are so closely related, some comment should first be made by way of clarification. First, the Gospel gives the revelation of the message *historically;* the Epistle gives it as *realized in Christian experience.* The key verses of the Gospel (20:30, 31), stress the *fact* of eternal life; the key verse of the Epistle (5:13) stresses the *assurance* of eternal life.

Second, the Gospel interprets the life and works of Jesus in history; the Epistle makes clear the significance of His Person. In the Gospel, "the Word" who was made flesh (1:14) *did*

---

[8]The expression "private interpretation" (v. 20) applies not to the readers but to the writers of Scripture. These men were not the originators of truth but the vehicles by whom the Spirit spoke (v. 21).

certain things ("signs") to bring people to faith in Himself as the Messiah and the Son of God (20:30, 31); in the Epistle "the Word" is identified as the Son of God manifested to destroy the works of the Devil (3:8), the One linked inseparably with the Father (2:22, 23) and the Propitiation for the sins of mankind (2:2; 4:10). The difference, again, is in point of emphasis. It is the same glorious Person who is presented to the reader of both books.

Finally, there are many vocabulary terms which are common to both works. Some of the most outstanding are "the Word"; "beginning"; "to witness" (thirty-three times in the Gospel; six in the Epistle); "manifested"; "eternal life"; "joy fulfilled"; "to believe" (ninety-eight times in the Gospel; nine in the Epistle); "abide"; "begotten"; and "love." Both books deal with the same vital subject—*life*—the first showing how to obtain it, the second making clear how to enjoy it to the full.

Author

Although the First Epistle, along with the Second and Third, is anonymous, its striking similarities of vocabulary and style with the Gospel mark it as the work of the same writer,[9] and the evidence from tradition is early and strong.[10] In this book the writer's message of the love of God for His children and their response to that love is especially prominent. So it is that John has been called "the Apostle of love."

Date and Destination

The date of the Epistle is probably about the same as that of the Gospel, A.D. 85-90. It was apparently intended for the churches of the province of Asia primarily,[11] although its appeal, like that of the Gospel, is universal.

---

[9]Tenney, *The New Testament: An Historical and Analytical Survey* (Grand Rapids: Eerdmans, 1953), p. 393, states that if vocabulary and style are considered adequate for pronouncing judgment on authorship, these three short letters must be attributed to the same author who is the author of the Fourth Gospel.

[10]Thiessen, *Introduction to the New Testament* (Grand Rapids: Eerdmans, 1943), pp. 306, 307, lists the testimonies of the Church Fathers from Polycarp to Eusebius.

[11]Along with this suggestion, made by Westcott, the names of Palestine, Parthia and Corinth have been mentioned.

Purpose

Stated clearly at the end of the Epistle is the foremost purpose of the book, namely, to give the *assurance* of eternal life to those believing in Christ (5:13). There is, however, a companion purpose in the Epistle. John writes to define the nature of the person of Christ in the face of heretical teachings which were afflicting the Church near the end of the first century. The general name given to this teaching was Gnosticism, a religio-philosophic school which was basically characterized by the idea that only spirit was good and matter was evil. As in other Greek and Oriental religious systems, the Gnostics believed that one must free himself from the material world and be occupied alone with spirit. The way of escape, for the Gnostics, was the way of superior knowledge. By learning the mysterious secrets of the universe, the initiate of the cult could supposedly attain freedom.

With regard to the teachings of Christianity, the opposition of this heresy centered in the Person of Christ. Obviously, if matter (which involved the human body) was evil, God could not be "manifest in the flesh," else He would be defiled. Therefore, Christ's humanity was not real; the disciples only saw a phantom; He only "seemed to be" real. If, as others taught, Jesus was truly man, the "Christ-spirit" did not actually unite with Him, except for the brief time between the baptism and the crucifixion.[12] This was, therefore, a denial of His deity.

When one becomes aware of these prevalent false claims, many of John's statements in the First Epistle take on new meaning. John combats Docetism by his insistence on the reality of the humanity of Christ (1:1-3; 4:1-3). He inveighs against Cerinthianism by emphasizing the fact that Jesus is the Christ, the Son of God (1:3, 7; 2:22, 23; 3:23; 4:15; 5:1, 20). This Epistle should serve as a final answer to a heresy which persists until the present day.

---

[12]The former of these beliefs was called Docetism from the Greek word *dokeo*, "to seem (to be)"; the latter Cerinthianism, after the name of its champion, Cerinthus. Tradition informs us that John knew Cerinthus and regarded him as an enemy of the Gospel.

Outline

As John expounds on the subject of Christian fellowship, he states that the realization of such fellowship will bring fullness of joy (1:4). This forms the chief note of the Epistle. He deals with the family of God: God is our Father, we are His "little children," and there are certain relationships which should obtain between the Father and the children.

John's First Epistle does not have the form of a logical treatise on a particular subject. It is rather like a symphonic or spiral arrangement. Again and again he returns to his central theme. Hence, the outline which follows is simply suggestive of outstanding emphases in each major part of the book.

I.	Introduction: The Reality of Fellowship	1:1-4
II.	The Requirements for Fellowship	1:5-10
III.	The Victorious Character of Fellowship	2:1-17
IV.	The Enemies of Fellowship	2:18-29
V.	The Reasons for Fellowship	3:1-12
VI.	The Tests of Fellowship	3:13-24
VII.	The Discernment of Fellowship	4:1-6
VIII.	The Practice of Fellowship	4:7-21
IX.	The Foundation of Fellowship	5:1-12
X.	The Privileges of Fellowship	5:13-21

In the course of the exposition of his theme of the family of God, John refers often to "the Father." A study of this doctrine in the Epistle will help one to arrive at a proper understanding of the nature of God's Fatherhood.

1.	"The eternal *life*, which was with the Father"	1:2
2.	"Our fellowship is with the Father"	1:3
3.	"We have an advocate with the Father"	2:1
4.	"Ye know the Father"	2:13
5.	"The love of the Father is not in him"	2:15
6.	"For all that is in the world . . . is not of the Father"	2:16

7. "This is the antichrist, *even* he that denieth
   the Father and the Son"   2:22
8. "Hath not the Father . . . hath the Father"   2:23
9. "Ye also shall abide in the Son, and
   in the Father"   2:24
10. "Behold what manner of love the Father hath
    bestowed upon us"   3:1
11. "The Father hath sent the Son"   4:14

It will be readily observed that the majority of the forego-
ing references occur in the second chapter of the Epistle. The
two main areas of teaching in this chapter are 1) the Christian
and the world and 2) the Christian and the Antichrist. The
former concerns the children's relationship to the Father and
His love for them; the latter deals with the rightful place of
the Father in the life of His children. A denial of the Father
and the Son is a sign of the spirit of Antichrist.

The references may be grouped under three main headings:

1. The relationship between the Father and the Son: 1:2,
   3; 2:1, 22, 23, 24; 4:14
2. The relationship between the Father and the world (the
   evil world-system): 2:15, 16
3. The relationship between the Father and His children:
   2:13; 3:1

II JOHN

Author

The two Epistles which follow are closely linked to the
First Epistle and the Gospel of John by the vocabulary and general subject matter. In addition, the letters were associated with
the apostle John from the second century onward, though not
unanimously. Origen and Eusebius expressed doubts as to their
authenticity, but Clement and Dionysius of Alexandria attrib-
ted them to John.

Date and Destination

No hint of date is given in the books themselves. Because

of the factors mentioned above, they may be assigned to the same period as I John, about A.D. 85-90.

To whom was II John addressed? The expression "unto the elect lady and her children" has been explained in two major ways: 1) an individual named Electa or Kyria and her children; or 2) a church with its congregation.[13] It seems quite possible that this letter, together with III John, was sent along with the Gospel and First Epistle as a personal message.

Purpose

From verses six through eight it would seem that John wrote this Epistle to re-emphasize the need for walking in the truth and being aware of prevalent error. His desire was to discuss these matters more fully in a later personal visit (v. 12).

Outline

I. Salutation		1-3
II. Walking in the Truth		4-11
	1. The commandment of the Father	4-6
	2. The message of the deceivers	7-11
III. Conclusion		12, 13

III JOHN

Date and Destination

The final Epistle of John, written at the same time as the Second, was addressed to "Gaius the beloved" (v. 1). The name was a common one. "Gaius of Macedonia" appears in Acts 19:29, "Gaius of Derbe" in Acts 20:4, and "Gaius (of Corinth)" in Romans 16:23. These men were all friends of Paul. Whether one of them is to be seen here in III John 1 cannot be determined with certainty. He was apparently a leader in the church to which this Epistle was sent.

Purpose

This letter was sent for a twofold purpose: 1) to encourage

---

[13]The name Electa was suggested by Clement of Alexandria; Kyria by the late Syrian version; and a church by Jerome. Commentators are still divided on the matter.

Gaius in his Christian hospitality, and 2) to deal with Diotrephes, a self-appointed dictator who was attempting to excommunicate all who did not measure up to his personal standard.

Outline

I. Salutation   1

II. Prayer for Gaius' Health   2-4

III. Praise for Gaius' Hospitality   5-8

IV. Condemnation of Diotrephes' Policy   9-11

V. Commendation of Demetrius' Character   12

VI. Conclusion   13

JUDE

Author

The writer identifies himself as "Jude, a servant of Jesus Christ, and brother of James" (v. 1). He may, therefore, be linked with James, the writer of an Epistle, "the brother of the Lord" (Matt. 13:55; Gal. 1:19) and the leader of the Jerusalem Church. As he was an unbeliever during Jesus' earthly ministry (John 7:5), his conversion must have followed the resurrection and he is next seen as a participant in the prayer meeting in Acts 1:14. His manner of expression is similar to both James and Peter.

Date and Destination

One important factor in determining the date of Jude is its relationship to II Peter. The second chapter of Peter's Epistle is strikingly similar to the Epistle of Jude. If the two were written about the same time, Jude may be dated about A.D. 67 or 68. If, however, his reference in verse 17 implies the passage of a number of years, a later date is necessitated, possibly A.D. 80-85.

From the many references to Old Testament persons and places, it would seem that Jude addressed himself to a Jewish-Christian audience.[14]

---

[14]Lenski, however, assumes that the letter was sent to Gentile Christians, arguing from the destination of II Peter *op. cit.*, pp. 242-244, 607.

Purpose

Jude's statement of purpose is clearly and dramatically given in verse 3. He set about to write to his readers of their "common salvation" but was constrained instead to exhort them "to contend earnestly for the faith once for all delivered to the saints." Apparently false teachers were taking their toll and Jude, being guided to write in such a manner, pens this strong plea in an attempt to thwart these evil persons (v. 4).

Outline

I. Salutation	1, 2
II. Exhortation: Defense of the Faith	3, 4
III. Illustration: Departures from the Faith	5-16
IV. Admonition: Progress in the Faith	17-23
V. Conclusion: A Doxology	24, 25

Jude makes striking use of the Old Testament to illustrate the judgment of God against apostasy. A comparison with II Peter 2 here is enlightening:

II Peter 2	Jude
1.	1. Israel in the wilderness
2. The fallen angels	2. The fallen angels
3. The Flood	3. . . . .
4. Sodom and Gomorrah	4. Sodom and Gomorrah
5.	5. The way of Cain
6. The way of Balaam	6. The error of Balaam
7.	7. The gainsaying of Korah

The Old Testament references which Jude includes serve three important purposes:

1. They are used as examples to warn believers. In verse 5, Israel illustrates *unbelief;* in verse 6, the angels illustrate *disobedience;* in verse 7, Sodom and Gomorrah illustrate *uncleanness.*

2. They are used as examples to show the character of the

false teachers of Jude's day. In verses 9 and 10, Satan illustrates *blasphemy;* in verse 11, Cain illustrates *self-will,* Balaam illustrates *the love of money,* and Korah illustrates *presumption.*

3. They are used as examples of the judgment of God against the ungodly. This is summarized in verse 15.

The Old Testament citations fall into two possible classes: canonical books (vv. 5, 7, 11) and apocryphal books (vv. 9, 14, 15). Jude's apparent use of apocryphal literature, The Assumption of Moses, and the Book of Enoch, does not necessarily imply either that the books were considered canonical or that the events referred to are fictional. They could well be true incidents and are used by Jude as illustrations. Paul did the same type of thing when quoting from pagan writers (Acts 17:28; Titus 1:12).

Having completed his illustrations, Jude stresses the necessity for diligence in maintaining a sound Christian experience. In contrast to the false teachers, who are schismatic and sensual,[15] Christians are to build themselves up, pray in the Spirit, keep themselves in the love of God, and look for the mercy of the Lord (vv. 20, 21).

Suggested Readings
I AND II PETER

Blenkin, G .W. *The First Epistle General of Peter* in the *Cambridge Greek Testament.* Cambridge: the University Press, 1914.

Jowett, J. H. *The Epistles of Peter.* London: Hodder and Stoughton, 1905.

Selwyn, E. G. *The First Epistle of Peter.* London: Macmillan & Co., Ltd., 1952. Thorough introduction, commentary on the Greek text, and special essays.

Stibbs, A. M. *The First Epistle General of Peter,* with an Introduction by A. F. Walls, in the Tyndale New Testament Commentaries. Grand Rapids: Wm. B. Eerdmans Publishing Co., 1959.

---

[15]The word "sensual" means "natural" or "fleshly." It occurs in I Corinthians 2:14, "the natural man" who "receiveth not the things of the Spirit of God." It refers to that "soulish life" which energizes the physical body and is opposed to the new nature in the believer.

Thomas, W. H. G. *The Apostle Peter*. Grand Rapids: Wm. B. Eerdmans Publishing Co., 1946. Studies in the life and work of Peter.

McNab, A. *The General Epistles of Peter* in *The New Bible Commentary*. Grand Rapids: Wm. B. Eerdmans Publishing Co., 1953. Pages 1129-1150.

I, II, III JOHN

Candlish, R. S. *The First Epistle of John*. Grand Rapids: Zondervan Publishing House, n.d. (reprint).

Findlay, G. G. *Fellowship in the Life Eternal: An Exposition of the Epistles of St. John.* London: Hodder and Stoughton, n.d.

Plummer, A. *The Epistles of St. John* in the *Cambridge Greek Testament*. Cambridge: Cambridge University Press, 1938.

Westcott, B. F. *The Epistles of St. John*. Grand Rapids: Wm. B. Eerdmans Publishing Co., 1950. Greek text with added notes and essays.

JUDE

Coder, S. M. *Jude: The Acts of the Apostates*. Chicago: Moody Press, 1958. In the Colportage Library, 365.

Robertson, R. *The General Epistle of Jude* in *The New Bible Commentary*. Grand Rapids: Wm. B. Eerdmans Publishing Co., 1953. Pages 1161-1167.

CHAPTER 15

THE PROPHETICAL LITERATURE: REVELATION

Introduction

THE LAST OF THE CANONICAL BOOKS is probably also the most neglected book—of the New Testament at least. Perhaps this neglect is due to the fact that the book abounds in symbols, images, mysterious creatures and veiled expressions. Yet the title of the book itself, given in the opening statement, "The Revelation of Jesus Christ which God gave him . . . and he sent and signified it by his angel unto his servant John" (1:1), should serve to dispel some of the prevalent neglect. It purports to be "an unveiling," "an uncovering," "a revealing" rather than a concealing of the message which it contains. While this is not a formula which will solve every problem of the book, a reverent study of the contents in dependence on the divine Teacher will make possible a good degree of understanding of its message.

Background

Revelation is a book of the class of "apocalyptic" writings. It compares more nearly to the Book of Daniel than to any other canonical writing. Such books which purport to "reveal" or "unveil" the future were usually written in times of persecution and trial as a means of encouraging and stabilizing the faith of those who were oppressed.[1]

As is evident from the book itself, persecution had already begun among these churches or was at least impending. To Smyrna it was said "thou art about to suffer" and "tribulation ten days" was prophesied (2:10). In Pergamum, the place of "Satan's throne," Antipas had been martyred for his faith (2:

[1]For a helpful summary of the historical, social, religious and literary backgrounds of Revelation, see M. C. Tenney, *Interpreting Revelation* (Grand Rapids: Eerdmans, 1957), pp. 17-27.

13). Thyatira was warned of "great tribulation" (2:22). To Philadelphia, the promise of protection was given against "the hour of trial, that *hour* which is to come upon the whole world" (3:10).

These were days of danger and daring; days of moral and spiritual uncertainty. These were the days of the reigns of the Caesars. From the days of Augustus (30 B.C.-A.D. 14), the Pax Romana, the "peace of Rome," prevailed. For the first thirty years of her existence (c. A.D. 30-60), the Christian Church was considered only a sect of Judaism and was able to continue unmolested by the Roman government. But in the days of Nero (A.D. 54-68) the Church was branded as a *religio illicita* and the blame for the fire in Rome (A.D. 64) was shifted to the Christians. In those days, as in the reign of Domitian (A.D. 81-96), there were local persecutions. Apparently the apostle John fell victim to one of these and so was exiled to Patmos for the faith (1:9). Domitian himself claimed to be divine and demanded worship as *Dominus et Deus* ("Lord and God"). For his Christian subjects it was a choice between "Lord Caesar" or "Lord Jesus."

Author

As the book itself states, the name of the human author was John (1:1, 4, 9; 22:8). As no further explanation is added, it seems fairly certain that the writer must have been well enough known in the churches of the province of Asia so that no other Christian leader of that name would be confused with him.[2] According to early Church tradition it was John the apostle who wrote the book.

The problem, however, is complicated by the style and language of the book as compared with the Gospel and Epistles of John. While an explanation must be given for these obvious differences, it need not necessarily be one which precludes Johannine authorship. It has, in fact, simply led some to date

---

[2]Manley, *The New Bible Handbook* (Chicago: Inter-Varsity Fellowship, 1953), p. 408.

the book much earlier than the traditional dating, saying that John's Greek was less polished then. Others have posited the idea that John wrote Revelation himself but employed an amanuensis for the Gospels and Epistles.

Date and Destination

According to Irenaeus, John wrote the Book of the Revelation "towards the end of Domitian's reign." As this emperor reigned from A.D. 81-96, the book has been traditionally dated between A.D. 90-95. Because of the hostility which is reflected in the book, the days of Domitian would form a good setting, as the Church was beginning to feel the pressure of Roman persecution.

The alternate date suggested by a number of scholars is late in the reign of the emperor Nero. This position is based primarily on the language and style of the book together with the belief that the mysterious number (666) found in 13:18 is a veiled reference to Nero. But the qualities of the book may fit as well into the later period and, in addition, the earlier date lacks external attestation.

According to chapter 1, the book is addressed to the seven churches of the Roman province of Asia: Ephesus, Smyrna, Pergamum, Thyatira, Sardis, Philadelphia and Laodicea (1:4, 11). As may be observed from the earlier New Testament records, Ephesus was the most prominent of the seven, only the church of Laodicea being mentioned among the others (Col. 4:16).

Methods of Interpretation

By what method or methods of study is one to approach this book? What chronological setting does the book have? Four basic approaches have been used in the history of its interpretation and each of these must be briefly defined and evaluated.

1. *The Preterist Method.* To the interpreter of this school, Revelation was fulfilled in the events of the first century and has, therefore, no prophetic aspect remaining. The conflicts depicted in the book were those between the first century Church and the Roman empire. While this view makes Revelation very

relevant to the day in which it was written, it does not do justice to its stated prophetic character (1:3, 19; 22:18, 19).

2. *The Historicist Method.* This approach understands Revelation as a "picture book" of the history of the world from the first century until the end of the age. It goes beyond the limitations of the preterist approach and therefore does more justice to the prophecy of "the things which shall come to pass hereafter" (1:19; 4:1). The greatest weakness of the historicist school is the disagreement of what symbols in the book match what particular historical events throughout the centuries.

3. *The Futurist Method.* With the possible exception of chapters 1-3, the futurist method assigns the book to a period at the end of the age, most of it fitting into the time called "the great tribulation" which immediately precedes the second coming of Christ (19:11 ff.).[3] The phrases in 1:19 and 4:1, therefore, are understood to refer to the far-distant future. The events of the book, as in the previous methods, are considered to be historical incidents. The area of weakness in this approach is the tendency to divorce the book from its original setting and its relevance to the early churches.

4. *The Idealist Method.* In distinction from the three preceding views, the idealist school deals with spiritual realities rather than historical situations. The book, apart from depicting any identifiable historic events, relates to the agelong struggle between God and Satan, good and evil, the Church and pagan culture. In the light of the Biblical insistence on the activity of God in the realm of human history, this school too greatly emphasizes the symbolic elements and completely eliminates the predictive element.

Purpose

In the light of the statements of the book itself a twofold purpose may be suggested. First, the Revelation was written to encourage Christians in the face of persecution and testing. This seems clear in the letters addressed to the seven churches.

---

[3]Some futurists see in chapters 1-3 the letters to the seven churches of Asia a pictorial representation of seven eras or stages in the history of the Church. This is similar to the historicist approach, although to a lesser degree.

Second, the book gives a sketch of the divine program in history, with special reference to the end of the present age. This appears to be the chief emphasis of the latter part of the book.

Outline

One clear indication of the structure of the contents is the repetition of the phrase "in the Spirit" (1:9, 10; 4:1, 2; 17:1-3; 21:9, 10). The four visions which are thus introduced form a framework for the detailed events which follow. It should also be emphasized that the Christological aspect of the book is central. In the opening sentences the words, "The Revelation of Jesus Christ" (1:1), may be understood to mean that the Lord Himself is the *source* of what is given. He has revealed these things to John. Even if the verse is taken to mean that the revelation concerns Him (that He is the *object* of the message), He remains central.

I. Introduction	1:1-8
1. The Revealer	1:1
2. The human author	1:2
3. The blessing	1:3
4. The salutation	1:4-8
II. The First Vision: Christ and the Seven Churches	1:9—3:22
1. The glory of Christ revealed	1:9-20
2. The epistles of Christ recorded	2:1—3:22
a. To Ephesus	2:1-7
b. To Smyrna	2:8-11
c. To Pergamum	2:12-17
d. To Thyatira	2:18-29
e. To Sardis	3:1-6
f. To Philadelphia	3:7-13
g. To Laodicea	3:14-22
III. The Second Vision: Christ and the Earth-Judgments	4:1—16:21
1. The throne in Heaven	4:1-11
2. The Lamb and the sealed roll	5:1-14

An Analysis of the Letters to the Seven Churches of Asia

REVELATION 2—3

Church	Ephesus 2:1-7	Smyrna 2:8-11	Pergamum 2:12-17	Thyatira 2:18-29	Sardis 3:1-6	Philadelphia 3:7-13	Laodicea 3:14-22
Character of Christ	Sovereign Lord 2:1	Risen Lord 2:8	Warring Lord 2:12, 16	Judging Lord 2:18	Omniscient Lord 3:1	Authoritative Lord 3:7	Divine Lord 3:14
Commendation	Orthodoxy 2:2	Endurance 2:9	Faithfulness 2:13	Industry 2:19	(none)	Endurance 3:10	(none)
Condemnation	Coldness 2:4	(none)	False Teaching 2:14, 15	Unfaithfulness 2:20	Unreality 3:1	(none)	Lukewarmness 3:15, 16
Counsel	Remember, repent, repeat first works 2:5	Be watchful unto death 2:10	Repent 2:16	Repent; hold fast 2:22, 25	Be watchful; remember, repent 3:2, 3	Hold fast 3:11	Buy gold, garments, eyesalve 3:18, 19
Caution	Removal 2:5	(none)	War 2:16	Death 2:23	Invasion 3:3	(none)	Separation 3:16
Covenant with overcomer	Eat of the tree of life 2:7	Not hurt of the second death 2:11	Hidden manna, White stone, new name 2:17	Rulership; morning star 2:26-28	White garments; name kept and confessed 3:5	New position; new name 3:12	Share Christ's throne 3:21

3. The seven seals opened   6:1—8:5
    Parenthesis: The 144,000 Sealed   7:1-8
       The great multitude   7:9-17
4. The seven trumpets sounded   8:6—11:19
    Parenthesis: The Little Book   10:1-11
       The Temple   11:1, 2
       The Two Witnesses   11:3-13
5. The beasts and their warfare   12:1—14:20
    a. The great red Dragon   12:1-17
    b. The Beast from the sea   13:1-10
    c. The Beast from the earth   13:11-18
       Parenthesis: The 144,000   14:1-5
          Angelic messages   14:6-20
6. The seven bowls poured out   15:1—16:21
    a. The scene in Heaven   15:1-8
    b. The judgments on the earth   16:1-21
IV. The Third Vision: Christ and
His Victories   17:1—21:8
   1. The fall of Babylon the Great   17:1—18:24
   2. The joy in Heaven   19:1-10
   3. The appearance of Christ   19:11-16
   4. The defeat of the Beast   19:17-21
   5. The binding of Satan   20:1-3
   6. The Millennium   20:4-6
   7. The final rebellion and judgment   20:7-15
   8. The new Heaven and the new earth   21:1-8
V. The Fourth Vision: Christ and
His Bride   21:9—22:5
   1. The New Jerusalem described   21:1-21
   2. The New Jerusalem and the earth   21:22-27
   3. The New Jerusalem and the new life   22:1-5
VI. Conclusion: Final Exhortations and
Benediction   22:6-21

In the first vision (1:9 ff.) John is overcome by the appearance of the glorified Christ, the Lord of life and death (1:18). It may be remembered that John was the closest of all the disciples to Jesus. He it was who leaned on Jesus' breast at the

The Three Series of Judgments

	Seal Judgments	Trumpet Judgments	Vial Judgments
1	6:1, 2 Rider on a white horse Carried a bow Wore a crown *Object:* To conquer	8:7 Hail, fire and blood on the earth *Result:* ⅓ part earth, ⅓ part trees, all green grass burned up	16:2 Poured into earth *Result:* Noisome and grievous sore upon worshipers of the beast
2	6:3, 4 Rider on a red horse Carried a great sword *Object:* To take peace from the earth	8:8, 9 Fiery mountain cast into the sea *Result:* ⅓ of sea blood, ⅓ of sea creatures die, ⅓ of ships destroyed	16:3 Poured into the sea *Result:* All sea-life died
3	6:5, 6 Rider on a black horse Carried a balance *Object:* Produce famine conditions	8:10, 11 Burning star falls upon earth—named Wormwood *Result:* ⅓ of waters made bitter; many men die	16:4-7 Poured in rivers and sources of waters *Result:* Water became blood; Revenge on murderers
4	6:7, 8 Rider on a pale horse Death followed by Hades *Object:* To kill by sword, famine, death and wild beasts	8:12 Celestial disturbances *Result:* ⅓ of heavenly bodies darkened; day and night affected	16:8, 9 Poured upon the sun *Result:* Men scorched with fire; blasphemed God
5	6:9-11 Souls of martyrs under the altar *Object:* To cry for revenge against their murderers	9:1-11 Star (ruler) falls to earth; opens the pit; locusts emerge led by Apollyon *Result:* Men tormented 5 months; unable to die	16:10, 11 Poured upon the throne of the beast *Result:* Kingdom darkened; men in pain; did not repent
6	6:12-17 Seismic and celestial disturbances *Object:* Day of God's wrath upon the earth	9:13-22 Four angels at Euphrates released; armies of horsemen proceed *Result:* ⅓ of men killed by horses which breathe fire, smoke and brimstone	16:12-16 Poured upon Euphrates River *Result:* River dried up. Eastern kings advance to Har-Magedon (Armagedon)
7	8:1, 2 Silence in heaven for a half-hour *Object:* Preparation for sounding of seven trumpets	11:15-19 Great voices in Heaven, and 24 elders sing praise to God *Result:* God's kingdom supreme over the earth	16:17-21 Poured upon the air *Result:* Voice announces "It is done"; disturbances and plague of hail; men blaspheme God

Last Supper; of him it was said that he was the disciple "whom Jesus loved." Yet on this occasion the sight of his Lord causes him to fall at His feet "as one dead" (1:17).

Each of the letters of Jesus to the churches is relevant first to the local situation, then to the lives of other believers who find themselves in similar circumstances. The accompanying chart will make clear the message to each church. It may be stressed here that to Smyrna and Philadelphia no condemnation is included; and only these two churches survive to the present day. Four things, at least, characterize each of the two letters:

1. Commendation; no condemnation (2:9; 3:8, 10)
2. The synagogue of Satan and false Jews (2:9; 3:9)
3. The warning of tribulation (2:10; 3:10)
4. The mention of crowns (2:10; 3:11)

The letters to Sardis and Laodicea, on the other hand, contain no commendation but only condemnation.

The three series of judgments in the second vision—the seven seals, the seven trumpets and the seven bowls—describe forcefully the judgments of God against those "that dwell upon the earth." Despite the ferocity of these events man remains unrepentant. This is stressed near the end of each series of events (6:15-17; 9:20, 21; 16:9, 11, 21).[4]

The two visions which conclude the book stand in vivid contrast. One centers in the harlot, the other in the Bride (17:1; 21:9). The former is a scene of immorality; the latter of purity. Babylon goes down to destruction; the Bride is triumphant.

With the defeat of the forces of evil God reigns supreme. The three chief enemies of God in the book are represented as 1) the dragon (chap. 12), 2) the first Beast, the Antichrist (13:1-10) and 3) the second Beast, the False Prophet (13:11-18). Christ, appearing as the Victor in 19:11-16, defeats the Beast

---

[4]The similarities of the judgments of the trumpets and vials should also be carefully noted: 1) the earth, 8:7; 16:2; 2) the sea, 8:8; 16:3; 3) the rivers and fountains, 8:10; 16:4; 4) the sun, 8:12; 16:8; 5) the abyss and Abaddon; the throne of the beast, 9:11; 16:10; 6) the Euphrates river, 9:14; 16:12; 7) voices and thunders, 11:15, 19; 16:17, 18.

and the False Prophet and consigns them to their doom (19:19-21.) Satan, being bound "for a thousand years" (20:2), is finally defeated and shares the fate of his companions in eternal torment (20:10).

Suggested Readings

Ladd, G. E. *Crucial Questions about the Kingdom of God.* Grand Rapids: Wm. B. Eerdmans Publishing Co., 1952. Chapters VII and VIII are a treatment of the problem of the Millennium in Revelation 20.

Ramsay, W. M. *The Letters to the Seven Churches of Asia and Their Place in the Plan of the Apocalypse.* Fourth Edition. London: Hodder and Stoughton, n.d.

Scott, W. *Exposition of the Revelation of Jesus Christ.* London: Pickering & Inglis, n.d.

Stauffer, E. *Christ and the Caesars:* Historical Sketches. Philadelphia: Westminster Press, 1955.

Stott, J. R. W. *What Christ Thinks of the Church.* Grand Rapids: Wm. B. Eerdmans Publishing Co., 1958. Messages on Revelation 1-3.

Swete, H. B. *The Apocalypse of St. John.* Third edition. London: Macmillan and Co., Limited, 1911. Full introduction. Commentary on the Greek text.

Tatford, F. A. *Prophecy's Last Word.* London: Pickering & Inglis, Ltd., 1947.

Tenney, M. C. *Interpreting Revelation.* Grand Rapids: Wm. B. Eerdmans Publishing Co., 1957. Analysis and topical studies. Bibliography. Highly recommended.

INDEX OF PERSONS AND PLACES

Aaron, 137, 140
Abaddon, 171
Abraham, 7, 14, 23, 43, 51, 95, 97, 101, 145
Achaia, 60, 61, 63, 65, 76, 82, 89
Adam, 43, 101
Adonis, 11
Aegean Sea, 74, 89
Agabus, 60
Alexander the Great, 9, 10, 58, 118, 143
Alexandria, 9, 111, 143
Ananias, 56
Ancyra, 93
Annas, 49
Antioch of Pisidia, 38, 60, 61, 66, 72, 82, 93, 94
Antioch of Syria, 21, 24, 60, 61, 70, 72, 82, 96, 142, 143
Antiochus IV Epiphanes, 8, 9
Antipas, 163
Apollos, 84, 135
Apollyon, 170
Aquila, 82, 99
Arabia, 70, 72
Archelaus, 7
Archippus, 108
Aristarchus, 60
Aristotle, 10
Asia, 60, 61, 63, 65, 105, 109, 110, 131, 148, 154, 165
Asia Minor, 11, 37, 61, 63, 93, 105, 148
Asiarchs, 56
Athens, 57, 60, 65, 73, 74, 87
Augustus Caesar, 11, 40, 111, 164

Balaam, 160, 161
Barnabas, 32, 36, 57, 60, 61, 63, 70, 72, 94, 128, 130, 134
Berea, 60, 65, 73, 74, 92
Bethany, 41
Bethlehem, 11
Bithynia, 63, 148

Cain, 160, 161
Caesarea, 20, 37, 54, 58, 59, 60, 65, 70, 73, 105
Cappadocia, 148
Carthage, 11, 142, 151
Cephas, 84, 147

Cerinthus, 155
Chalcis, 8
Chloe, 83
Cilicia, 60, 63, 72
Colossae, 105, 107
Corinth, 56, 60, 61, 65, 66, 73, 74, 75, 77, 82, 83, 84, 85, 86, 88, 89, 90, 91, 92, 98, 99, 118, 128, 143, 154
Cornelius, 57
Crete, 122, 128
Crispus, 61
Cybele, 11
Cyprus, 56, 60, 61, 63, 72

Dalmatia, 128
Damaris, 60
Damascus, 70, 72
David, 14, 23, 25, 27
Decapolis, 34
Demas, 37
Demetrius, 111, 159
Derbe, 60, 63, 66, 72, 93, 94, 125
Diana (Artemis) 110, 111
Dionysius, 60, 61
Diotrophes, 159
Dives, 41
Domitian, 164, 165

Egypt, 9, 11
Elymas, 60
Emmaus, 40, 42, 43
Epaphras, 37, 105
Epaphroditus, 118, 119
Ephesus, 21, 56, 60, 65, 66, 73, 74. 82, 88, 89, 98, 99, 105, 106, 109, 110, 111, 122, 124, 125, 143, 165
Epicurus, 10
Ethiopia, 59
Eutychus, 60

Felix, 56, 65
Festus, 56, 65

Gabriel, 42
Gaius, 158, 159
Gaius (of Corinth), 158
Gaius (of Derbe), 60, 125, 158
Gaius (of Macedonia), 158
Galatia, 60, 61, 63, 73, 90, 93, 94, 96, 148

Galilee, 7, 18, 25, 33, 34, 39, 40, 41
Gallio, 12, 56, 60, 82
Gamaliel, 69
Garden of Gethsemane, 35, 40, 148
Gaza, 59
Gomorrah, 160
Greece, 11, 60, 73

Har-Magedon, 170
Hellas, 10
Herod Agrippa I, 8, 96
Herod Agrippa II, 8, 56, 65
Herod Antipas, 7
Herod the Great, 7, 11, 40
Hierapolis, 105

Iconium, 38, 60, 61, 66, 72, 93, 94
Indus River, 9
Isaac, 97
Isaiah, 40
Ishmael, 97
Italy, 136

Jacob, 46
Jairus, 148
James, 15, 16, 38, 57, 63, 96, 134,
    141-145, 148
James (son of Zebedee), 47, 91, 96,
    141
Jerusalem, 7, 8, 12, 20, 21, 24, 27,
    29, 30, 32, 34, 39, 41, 42, 46, 55,
    57-60, 65, 70, 72-74, 88, 92-94,
    99, 105, 128, 136, 142-143
Jesus Justus, 36
John the Apostle, 15, 16, 18, 19, 21,
    32, 38, 46, 47, 48, 49, 50, 52, 59,
    91, 96, 148, 153-158, 163-171
John the Baptizer, 8, 11, 12, 25, 27,
    39, 40, 42, 49
Joppa, 59
Jordan, 41
Joseph, 11
Josephus, 7
Joshua, 137, 140
Judah, 43
Jude, 15, 16, 141, 159-161
Judea, 8, 11, 12, 18, 34, 40, 41, 55,
    57, 59
Julius Caesar, 82
Jupiter (Zeus), 61, 110

Korah, 160, 161

Laodicea, 105, 109, 151, 165, 171
Lazarus, 41, 43
Lazarus of Bethany, 51
Levi (Matthew), 24
Luke, 11, 15, 16, 19, 20, 32, 36, 37,
    38, 40, 42, 54, 55, 56, 58, 60, 61,
    65, 74, 82, 94, 118, 124, 128, 130,
    135

Lydia, 60, 61, 117
Lystra, 38, 60, 61, 63, 66, 72, 93,
    94, 125

Macedon, 9
Macedonia, 37, 60, 61, 63, 65, 73,
    74, 76, 89, 92, 98, 117, 118
Mark, 15, 19, 32, 33, 34, 35, 36, 60,
    61, 63, 108, 130
Mars' Hill, 60
Martha, 43, 52
Mary, 11, 39, 40, 42
Mary of Bethany, 43, 52
Matthew, 15, 16, 19, 23, 24, 25, 28,
    30, 32
Mediterranean, 11, 83, 111
Melchizedek, 140
Mercury (Hermes), 61
Michael, 161
Miletus, 10, 60, 65, 73
Mithras, 11
Moses, 28, 137, 140
Mount of Olives, 42
Mummius, 82

Nazareth, 24, 25, 40, 70
Nero Caesar, 37, 65, 70, 79, 104,
    148, 151, 164, 165
Nicodemus, 49, 52

Onesimus, 72, 105, 108, 115, 116,
    133

Palestine, 7, 8, 11, 18, 26, 46, 59,
    143, 154
Pamphylia, 60, 61
Paphos, 60
Parthia, 154
Paul, 15, 16, 19, 20, 21, 30, 36, 37,
    38, 54, 55, 56, 57, 60, 61, 63, 66,
    69-133, 134, 135, 145, 150, 151
Perea, 34, 39, 41
Perga, 60, 72
Pergamum, 65, 110, 163
Persia, 9, 11
Pessinus, 93
Peter, 15, 16, 19, 20, 21, 30, 32, 44,
    47, 50, 56, 57, 58, 59, 94, 96, 99,
    130, 143, 147-153
Pharisees, 8, 9, 27, 41
Philadelphia, 164, 171
Philemon, 72, 105, 115, 116, 133
Philip of Macedon, 9, 118
Philip (the Evangelist), 57, 59
Philippi, 36, 56, 60, 61, 65, 66, 73,
    74, 83, 89, 92, 117, 118
Phoebe, 99, 127
Phoenicia, 9, 11
Phrygia, 60, 105
Pilate, 7, 8, 12, 27, 49, 50, 52
Plato, 10

Pompey, 7, 8
Pontus, 148
Priscilla, 82, 99
Ptolemais, 60

Rome, 7, 11, 20, 32, 33, 37, 54, 55,
    65, 70, 73, 99, 102, 104, 105, 115,
    117, 125, 130, 136, 142, 148, 164

Sadducees, 8
Salamis, 60
Samaria, 41, 55, 57, 59
Sapphira, 56
Sardis, 171
Satan, 40, 75, 85, 161, 163, 166,
    169, 171, 172
Saul of Tarsus, 9, 57, 59, 61, 69, 70
Sceva, 111
Secundus, 60
Seleucia, 60
Seneca, 79, 82
Serapis, 11
Sergius Paulus, 55, 60, 61
Seven Churches of Asia, 165, 167,
    168
Silas, 56, 60, 61, 63, 74, 76, 117, 148
Siloam, 40
Simeon, 42
Simon (of Joppa), 59
Smyrna, 163, 171

Sodom, 160
Solomon, 23, 46
Sopater, 60
Stephen, 57, 58, 59, 70
Sychar, 46
Syria, 8, 60, 63

Tarsus, 69, 70, 72
Tavium, 93
Thales, 10
Theophilus, 37, 38, 54
Thessalonica, 60, 65, 66, 73, 74, 76,
    77, 78, 92, 118
Thomas, 18, 49, 52
Thyatira, 164
Tiberius Caesar, 12, 40
Timothy, 36, 38, 60, 61, 63, 65, 74,
    75, 76, 89, 94, 119, 122, 125-128,
    130-132, 135, 136, 150
Titus, 91, 92, 122, 128, 129
Troas, 36, 60, 63, 65, 73, 74, 89, 117
Trophimus, 60
Tychicus, 60, 105, 108, 115
Tyre, 60

Zacchaeus, 43
Zacharias, 11, 39, 40, 42
Zebedee, 47, 148
Zeno, 10
Zerubbabel, 143

INDEX OF AUTHORS

Alexander, J. A., 35
Alford, H., 6
Arndt and Gingrich, 76, 91

Barrett, C. K., 13
Bernard, J. H., 133
Blaiklock, E. M., 16, 67
Blenkin, G. W., 161
Broadus, J. A., 31
Bruce, A. B., 120
Bruce, F. F., 13, 16, 37, 68, 106,
    107, 118, 121, 131
Buttrick, G. A., 6

Cadbury, H. J., 67
Candlish, R. S., 162
Chafer, L. S., 29
Clement of Alexandria, 46, 135, 158
Coder, S. M., 162
Conybeare and Howson, 69, 79, 93

Danby, H., 69
Davidson, F., 6
Davies, W. D., 108

Edersheim, A., 21
Eusebius, 24, 46

Fairbairn, P., 133
Fairweather, W., 13, 79
Farrar, F. W., 135
Findlay, G. G., 162
Foakes-Jackson, F. J., 67

Geldenhuys, N., 41, 45
Godet, F. L., 45, 52, 103
Goodspeed, E. J., 31
Goodwin, F. J., 67
Green, J. B., 137
Grosheide, F. W., 103
Guthrie, D., 122, 123, 133

Hayes, D. A., 52, 79, 89, 104, 110,
    115, 117, 122, 123, 133, 146
Hendriksen, W., 52, 75, 78, 80, 122,
    123, 133
Hiebert, D. E., 79, 110, 111, 124,
    126
Hogg and Vine, 79, 80, 103
Hunter, A. M., 35

Irenaeus, 32, 164

Jerome, 158
Jowett, J. H., 161

Kent, H. A., 133
Kevan, E. F., 6
King, G. H., 31, 133, 146

Ladd, G. E., 29, 172
Lake, K., 67
Lang, G. H., 145
Lange, J. P., 6
Lenski, R. C. H., 6, 127, 145, 152, 159
Lightfoot, J. B., 93, 103, 106, 107, 116, 120, 121
Luce, H. K., 45

Macaulay, J. C., 52, 68
Machen, J. G., 21, 79
Manley, G. T., 13, 18, 77, 90, 136, 164
Marcion, 122
Mayor, J. G., 146
McNab, A., 162
Metzger, B. M., 13, 129
Milligan, G., 74, 78, 80
Moffat, 135
Moorehead, W. G., 68, 146
Morgan, G. C., 21, 31, 35, 68, 103
Morris, L., 21, 80
Moule, H. C. G., 103, 120
Moulton and Milligan, 74, 116
Murray, A., 145

Newell, W. R., 103
Nicoll, W. R., 6

Origen, 135
Orr, James, 16

Papias, 24, 46
Perowne, S., 13
Pfeiffer, C. F., 13
Pfeiffer, R. H., 13
Plummer, A., 31, 45, 85, 103, 162
Proctor, W. C. G., 92
Purves, G. T., 67

Rackham R. B., 55, 57, 68
Ramsay, W. M., 65, 67, 73, 93, 94, 110, 111, 172

Rees, P. S., 121
Rees, T., 135, 136
Ridderbos, H., 79, 93
Robertson, A., 85, 103
Robertson, A. T., 6, 32, 35, 55
Robertson, R., 162
Robinson, J. A., 110, 121

St. John, H., 35
Sanday, W., 21
Sauer, E., 13, 145
Schaff, P., 21, 85
Scott, E. F., 17, 37, 46, 90, 93, 123, 124, 136
Scott, W., 172
Scroggie, W. G., 17, 21, 23, 25, 28, 32, 34, 43, 90, 109, 130, 134
Selwyn, E. G., 148, 161
Simpson, E. K., 106, 107, 110, 121, 123, 133
Smith, D., 53, 79, 87, 105, 111, 123, 126, 131
Snaith, N. H., 13
Stalker, J., 79
Stauffer, E., 172
Stendahl, K., 108
Stibbs, A. M., 6, 161
Stonehouse, N. B., 6, 31, 41, 42
Stott, J. R. W., 172
Strauss, L., 146
Streeter, B. H., 35
Swete, H. B., 35, 78, 172

Tatford, F. A., 172
Tenney, M. C., 13, 21, 50, 51, 53, 88, 89, 93, 103, 105, 117, 120, 121, 125, 128, 132, 136, 142, 154, 164, 172
Thayer, J. H., 52
Thiessen, H. C., 17, 19, 33, 37, 90, 154
Thomas, W. H. G., 45, 53, 103, 145, 162
Twilley, L. D., 17

Vincent, M., 6, 121

Westcott, B. F., 46, 54, 121, 136, 146, 154, 162
Williams, A. L., 121
Wright, G. E., 110